What Others Are Saying About
Chris Gethard and *A Bad Idea I'm About to Do*

"Chris Gethard is comedy in a fighter's crouch. His stories travel through adolescence and New Jersey with a sweetness and rage that makes you both wish you were there and feel like you were."
— Seth Meyers, *Saturday Night Live*

"Whenever I'm feeling down on myself or think that I'm slowly going crazy, I think of one of Gethard's stories. Then I realize that, hey, I don't got it so bad after all."
— Jack McBrayer, *30 Rock*

"Chris Gethard tells the amazing stories an eccentric old man would tell . . . if that man had lived his fucking life with any balls. His stories are hilarious and riveting—but more importantly, real."
— Rob Huebel, Adult Swim's *Childrens Hospital*
and MTV's *Human Giant*

"Chris Gethard stories are like a roller coaster—at times you are scared, shocked, and ultimately exhilarated by the hilarity each story contains—and once you finish one, you wanna hear another one right away."
— Paul Scheer, FX's *The League* and Adult Swim's *NTSF: SD: SUV*

"Chris Gethard is one of my favorite storytellers. He's amazing! He's always getting into the most unusual situations. . . . Even normal situations become amazing when you're Chris Gethard. Seriously, when Geth is talking, I stop and listen."
— Rob Riggle, *The Daily Show with Jon Stewart*

"Maybe you shouldn't tell me things like that."
— Chris's mom responding to the distressing news that her son might have herpes

A BAD IDEA
I'M ABOUT TO DO

A BAD IDEA I'M ABOUT TO DO

TRUE TALES OF SERIOUSLY POOR JUDGMENT AND STUNNINGLY AWKWARD ADVENTURE

CHRIS GETHARD

DA CAPO PRESS
A Member of the Perseus Books Group

Copyright © 2012 by Chris Gethard

Designed by Trish Wilkinson
Set in 11 point Minion by The Perseus Books Group

Library of Congress Cataloging-in-Publication Data

Gethard, Chris.
    A bad idea I'm about to do : true tales of seriously poor judgment and stunningly awkward adventure / Chris Gethard.—1st Da Capo press ed.
        p.   cm.
    ISBN 978-0-306-82030-4 (pbk. : alk. paper); ISBN: 978-0-306-82059-5 (e-book) 1. American wit and humor. I. Title.
PN6165.G48 2011
818'.602—dc23   2011037223

First Da Capo Press edition 2012

Published by Da Capo Press
A Member of the Perseus Books Group
www.dacapopress.com

Da Capo Press books are available at special discounts for bulk purchases in the U.S. by corporations, institutions, and other organizations. For more information, please contact the Special Markets Department at the Perseus Books Group, 2300 Chestnut Street, Suite 200, Philadelphia, PA 19103, or call (800) 810-4145, ext. 5000, or e-mail special.markets@perseusbooks.com.

10 9 8 7 6 5 4 3 2 1

To my mother and my Aunt Re,
who while sitting at my kitchen table and
talking into the night taught me that sad stories
stop being sad if you can make them funny.

Contents

Introduction

"Would you like to hear a story I've never told anyone?" my mother asked.

We were in the living room of my parents' home in New Jersey. My mother sat in her familiar spot on the couch. My dad was at the kitchen table.

It was Mother's Day 2010.

Foolishly, I said "Sure."

"Great," she began. "It's about your birth."

My father interrupted as he entered from the other room. "And I've never heard it?"

"No," she said. She paused, looked at me, and continued. "I've never had the heart to tell anyone this story."

That's the moment it first hit me that when your mother asks you if you want to hear a story no one's ever heard, you should probably always say "No."

"When you were little and the other kids used to make fun of how big your head was," she told me, "it always broke my heart."

This meant her heart was broken nearly every single day. My forehead has always been an obtrusive, disproportioned source of embarrassment to me. My childhood nickname was "Megahead." (In many ways this was a good thing. While "Megahead" made me angry, I preferred it to being mocked about how my last name phonetically spells out the words "Get Hard.")

"I knew since day one that was going to be a problem for you," she continued. "Because when you were being born and you started crowning—you know, emerging? The doctor took a step back and said, 'My God, his head is as big as a bowling ball.'"

I froze.

That's how my life began, I thought to myself. *That's literally the first thing that ever happened to me. It wouldn't even be fair to measure my life in units of time yet. I was only three inches old and I was being mocked by the medical care professional whose job it was to bring me into life safely.*

My mom had obviously thought I would laugh at this story. When she saw that instead I was reeling from it, she tried to make a joke to recover.

"Well," she sighed, "you'll never know how many stitches they gave me."

Her joke didn't make me feel any better.

"How many?" I asked. I was approaching full panic.

She got very serious as she realized she was digging herself into a deeper hole.

"No, seriously, you'll never know," she said. "They refused to tell me."

That pushed me over the edge. "Jesus, I'm sorry!" I spat out.

I have to say, apologizing to your mother on Mother's Day for being born is not one of life's peaks. That can safely be described as a valley.

Before I could say anything, my father jumped in with his own attempt at a joke meant to save the situation.

"Actually," he said, "you should be apologizing to *me* for that." That's how I spent last Mother's Day.

~~~

That story verifies a suspicion I've long held—that my life has always been semi-ridiculous. Having lived the kind of life I've lived, I wasn't surprised at all to find out that's apparently been the case literally from the start. It figures that even my birth would be weird.

On paper, I appear to have it made. Everything about my upbringing seems to subscribe to the good old American dream. Raised in the suburbs, parents still married, good grades—if anyone should have had it easy, boring, and normal, it's me.

But right from the start I was perceptive enough to recognize that the traditional idea of a "normal life" doesn't really exist. There are cracks in its armor that anyone can see from a mile away. For example, the seemingly idyllic suburb I was raised in was actually filled with maniacal weirdos. My unfractured family in fact put on stunning displays of rage and lunacy. From a very early age, I'd see and experience things that would make me think *This isn't right* and *I have a feeling life is in general more messed up than anyone is letting on*. This type of thinking bred into me an unfortunate blend of curiosity and defiance.

What I've come to realize is that most people, when faced with a situation that seems ludicrous or dangerous, instinctually take action to avoid it. I, on the other hand, have always wanted to charge headlong into outlandish situations at first sight of them. The weirder something is, the more I want to know about it. The less likely it is for a guy like me to be a part of something, the more I want to get involved. My philosophy has always been "Why say no to anything?" The only things you have to abandon in order to live by it are common sense, a command of reason, and social acceptability. Not a bad trade.

In the early part of this book, you'll see what I mean about the foundation that my early life laid out for me. I'd wager that if you had the same male role models I did, you wouldn't quite know how life is supposed to work, either. By the time I describe my adventures as a young adult, you'll have learned how I'd developed a personality that got me into car chases, prison (voluntarily), and many other ill-advised pursuits. Then you'll see how things only snowballed from there.

Sometimes when I tell people these stories, I get the feeling they think I'm crazy. Over the years, I've come to realize that they're probably at least a little bit right.

But to me, it always seemed that everything and everyone *around* me was crazy, and that not embracing or addressing that realization would actually make me the weird one. Pretending everything was okay all the time, when life is so odd and often so harsh, seemed more damaging than not.

As a result, I've made a lot of foolish decisions. Many people hear about the stuff I've pulled and call me an angry person. The stories you are about to read will definitely reflect that. Others have called me depressed, and I am unable to argue with that diagnosis. Still others have viewed me as standoffish or socially awkward. I'm probably guilty on all counts.

But I don't think any of those individual labels hit the nail on the head. To me, they're mere extensions of what I really am and always have been—confused.

Just terribly, terribly confused. About why things work the way they do and why we all pretend that things aren't weird in one way or another *almost all the time.*

Unless, of course, it's just me.

But, listen, I'm working on this impulse of mine to dive into the middle of situations both awkward and strange.

Less than two weeks ago, I took the R train from my neighborhood in Queens into Manhattan. It was early afternoon on a Wednesday. At first, everything about the experience was perfectly average.

As I sat in the largely empty subway car, I had my face buried in my BlackBerry, because lately I've been addicted to playing poker on it. This activity helps pass the time, and also helps me maintain the social norm of public transportation in New York City, which is to never make eye contact with anyone, ever.

"EXCUSE ME LADIES AND GENTLEMEN, I NEED A MOMENT OF YOUR TIME," I heard from the other end of the car. This is not an unusual sentence to hear on a New York City subway. But the aggression and volume put into this particular delivery caused me to look up wide-eyed.

At the other end of the car, the homeless guy responsible for the disruption prepared to launch into his spiel. He didn't look particularly crazy by the standards of New York City homeless people. But he soon proved that looks can be deceiving.

Apparently, I was not the only person to react to him with surprise.

"Oh, this cunt doesn't have the time for me!" the homeless gentleman continued. "Bitch gonna roll her eyes at me."

"Cunt" is one of the few words that can slice through the thickest of skin. At the very least, it makes any situation more awkward than it was before. I was born and raised in New Jersey, where profanity is considered a quaint regional dialect. Now I live in New York City, where just days ago I witnessed two women going for the same taxi.

"Fuck you, bitch," yelled the woman who lost. "Karma will fuck you in the face."

That didn't faze me at all. Most things don't. But for some reason the word "cunt" still does.

The impact of the word was even more pronounced when I saw the woman he had directed it to spring out of her seat and head toward my end of the car. Imagine *anyone's grandma*. She was tiny, her white bushy hair slightly unkempt, her too-large purse balanced precariously in the crook of her arm as she fled from the madman who had just screamed "cunt" in her perfect little grandma face.

She hurried past me and sat down in the far corner of the car. The homeless guy continued.

"Ladies and gentlemen, I am here today to ask for donations," he said, "so I can pursue my dream . . . of being a *professional wrestler*."

At that point my internal monologue went into overdrive.

You don't get to call a woman a cunt, I thought to myself, *when you have the same fucking dream I had when I was nine years old.*

"I have wrestled in the independent leagues," he shouted as he headed in my direction, "but I need money to take more classes. Because there are still so many people I want to beat!"

I would sooner give you money if you were up there saying "Please give me money to support my heroin addiction," I thought. *It seems like a more direct route to exactly the same result.*

"With your help, I know I can be a world champion!" he bellowed.

Even in the world of professional wrestling, it's not okay to speak that way to women, I fumed to myself. *Even the scummiest wrestler on earth* (we can all agree that's Jake "The Snake" Roberts, right?) *would be like "Yo dude, cool out with the cunt shit."*

The man made his way past me. I didn't say anything. Despite all the indignation screaming to be let out from the depths of my psyche, I just kept playing poker on my smartphone.

I didn't feel that guilty. Other people actually *gave him money.*

But the thing is, a few years back I would absolutely have engaged this man in a dialogue. I can say with certainty that I would have confronted him about calling the old woman a cunt, and if that didn't lead to my being beaten on an underground train, I would then have eagerly asked him where he trained in the art of professional wrestling. And if this was actually something he did, I would have asked him to take me to his school. Because I desperately would have wanted to see a homeless wrestling school.

I know I would have done all of these things, because those are precisely my instincts even today. If there is a school out there where dozens of homeless people are jumping off ropes and landing on each other, it is something I absolutely need to experience firsthand. I can't tell you how hard it was for me not to confront that man on the train, but also not to ask him for every detail regarding his unlikely or, at best, confusing pursuit of fake fighting.

Instead, I bit my lip and lost a few more hands of mobile-phone poker. It's taken me thirty years of life, but I've finally discovered that normal people don't embrace craziness; they resist it. I didn't say a thing to the homeless wrestler. A few minutes later, I got off the train.

That's improvement, right?

In a sense, the stories you are about to read are about instances in my life when, rather than get off the train, I stayed on well past my stop. It's not that I'm anything special. I'm just your average geek trying to get by.

The only thing close to a remarkable quality I might claim to possess is that when most people would say no, I too often say yes. (I refer to this as a remarkable quality. Most people just call it stupidity.) It's an impulse that has certainly made life more interesting for me, but it's also been very detrimental at times.

Either way you view it, I hope the daring or idiocy described in these pages provides some cathartic relief for those of you who can think back to a situation where you may actually regret not taking a chance on what at the time seemed like a very bad idea. After all, my experiences confirm that, in most cases, people don't go out on a limb for a reason—straying outside of one's comfort zone is often dumb and causes trouble. By the end of the majority of these stories you'll likely feel good about not taking the road less socially advisable. Then again, sticking to the normal road can also be what leads us to the times we've all had when we wish we'd spoken up, but didn't; situations we look back on where we felt pushed around, forgotten, or inconsequential and wish we'd done something about it. So maybe these stories will also inspire you to take a chance in that regard. In any case, I hope that when you read these stories you can find something to relate to, take some kind of comfort in the fact that we've all been in strange situations—or, at the very least, realize that you could have made things so much worse.

It would make me feel a lot better if you did.

My Father Is Not the Kindly
Mustachioed Man He Seems

I'm obsessed with basketball. I'll drop anything to watch an NBA game. I'll watch summer league games. I'll watch old games on ESPN Classic. I'll even watch the Wizards play the Timberwolves.

I also love playing basketball, even though I'm not very good at it. Luckily, I've joined a team of comedians who are just as enthusiastic and equally bad. We're called The Del Harris Marathon, and what we lack in skill we make up for in dirty play and hilarious taunts. We're not the best, but we're gritty. We're part of a league that donates the dues teams pay to charity. My team plays for the March of Dimes, a noble organization if ever there was one.

The kind-hearted nature of this endeavor only makes my behavior during games that much less excusable.

Case in point: the third week of the season we played our rivals, The 4Skins. They're a bunch of Jewish guys who run set plays and are known for smothering defense. They're antisocial and cocky. We consider them our archenemies.

When we're playing The 4Skins, the chatter never stops.

"Nice cut, Ari!"

"Good hands, Harry!"

"He can't stop you, Goldie!"

One of them even plays in a protective facemask. They're just the worst. They get my anger up. And that's a problem.

I'm unable to tell you what it feels like to be "a little" mad. My emotions work as if controlled by a light switch. I'm either fine or I'm out of control. I once spilled a container of thumbtacks and got as angry at myself as I did when I screwed up my relationship with my high school sweetheart. If I'm under the impression that there are Golden Grahams in my cupboard, then realize that there in fact are none, there's a high probability I'll be as sad as I was at my grandfather's funeral.

In other words, my reactions aren't in proportion to the things I'm reacting to. It's something I've been working on with a very lovely shrink for the past few years.

But against The 4Skins one day, all that hard work went out the window.

Even in a charity basketball league, there are rules and those rules should be enforced. So I'm sorry, but if there is supposed to be a thirty-second shot clock and the ref doesn't seem to care, I'm going to enlighten him.

I was riding the bench with my friend Gavin, perhaps the nicest person I know.

"This is fucking bullshit," I seethed to him. "I've gotta say something."

"I don't know, man," he said. "Is it really worth it?"

I jumped off the bench and threw my hands wildly in the air.

"SHOT CLOCK," I screamed. "REF! WHAT ABOUT THE SHOT CLOCK!"

The ref ignored me.

"Why won't you pay attention to the FUCKING SHOT CLOCK?" I shouted.

"Dude," Gavin said. He shook his head, imploring me to calm down.

I stared at him with steely resolve before turning back in the ref's direction.

"Why do we even HAVE a fucking SHOT CLOCK?"

The ref blew his whistle.

I am the only player in the history of our charity sports league to be given a technical foul while on the bench.

~~~

My closest friends are all people who have learned to laugh at me during these types of situations. Otherwise, it would probably be impossible for them to tolerate my semi-frequent outbursts of completely uncalled-for emotion. They've figured out how to roll with these particular punches but have often wondered aloud where my anger comes from, and are generally shocked at my answer. Especially if they've met my parents.

For her part, my mother actually has no need to express outward anger, because she is very smart and skillfully passive-aggressive. My mother is Catholic, and that means she is a legitimate master of guilt inducement. I don't remember her ever yelling at me when I was growing up, but I do recall being on the business end of the following choice statements quite often:

"I thought I raised you better than that."

"I didn't realize that I was so terrible."

And worst of all: "I just didn't know you were that kind of person."

Usually, a heartbreaker of a line like that would be more than enough to put me in my place when I was acting out as a kid. But even when it didn't, she never resorted to screaming or yelling.

She'd simply say, "Okay . . . I'll just tell your father about this when he gets home."

Most people who meet my dad immediately like him. "He just seems like a nice guy," they'll say. "A nice guy with a moustache."

In addition to the moustache, his defining characteristics are that he's big (six foot two), slightly out of his element in social situations (but in an endearing way that's accompanied by a goofy grin), and a national expert on water treatment. When we go on vacation, his first order of business is to taste the tap water.

"Man, the pH is all off," he'll say, shaking his head. "I should go talk to these guys." You can't not love a guy who makes it his personal crusade to travel around America giving the locals slightly better drinking water.

My father's other interests include gardening, baking, and my mom. He's like the big quiet friend everyone wants in life. I don't feel cheesy saying I'm lucky he's my dad.

But like a suburban town that's home to a serial killer, or a likable athlete who runs a dog-fighting ring, my father has a dark side.

"Not *your* dad!" people say when I tell them my anger is inherited from him.

Then I recount a tale that has been passed down through my family for thirty years—a tale of a wronged man out for justice. A tale of vengeance. A tale of my father.

In August of 1980, I was three months old. My older brother was the tender age of two, and he was a bad sleeper. For my mom, this meant long sleepless nights that really took a toll on her. My father has always been incredibly protective of my mother, and seeing her exhausted and at the end of her rope made him even more so than usual.

My parents had recently moved into the first home they owned, on Franklin Avenue in West Orange, New Jersey. It was nothing fancy. There was no front lawn, so the modest house sat right up against the road. The cracked driveway led to a cramped backyard. The interior was the same: small and cozy, an admitted fixer-upper.

Both of my parents had grown up in the neighborhood and knew it well. The section of town it was located in was generally a good one, but had always had a rough element. Up the street was Colgate Park. For generations it had been a meeting ground for teenage kids—specifically, the type who liked to cause trouble—and around this time there was a notorious crew of burnouts who called the park their home base.

My father became obsessed with launching into home improvement projects. This is how he's been with every home he's owned since. It pains him to hire anyone to do something he can do with his own hands. I think this gives him the sense that these houses aren't just random buildings anymore—they're really his.

That's probably why the door was such a big deal.

The first alteration he made to the house on Franklin Avenue was to install a shiny, white aluminum door. After all, this was the brand-new entrance to his brand-new home. It was the literal gateway that would welcome visitors into the biggest and most important purchase he had ever made.

Perhaps that helps explain the vigilante death spree my father embarked upon.

A few nights after the door was proudly hung on its hinges, my parents were awakened at two in the morning by a terrifying crash. My brother woke from a rare night of sound sleep and screamed. I was up and crying as well. My father ran downstairs to discover that someone had kicked in his brand-new door. The first personal touch he put on his house had been destroyed.

The next morning he got up and removed the battered door from its hinges. He took a hammer and went through the arduous process of flattening it into as much of its original shape as possible, and rehung it. But it was no longer pristine. It was no longer new. His home—*his* home—already had its first blemish.

That night, the door was kicked in again. The results were the same: his months-old newborn screaming in fear. The baby's two-year-old brother crying in confusion. The babies' frazzled mother awake all night. And in the midst of all this frenzy my beleaguered father, who had to get up for work at the crack of dawn so he could feed the family that he felt he was currently failing to protect. Not to mention he was going to have to hammer out and rehang the goddamn aluminum door that some neighborhood kids found so hilariously kick-in-able.

This happened every night for the next four nights.

Maybe you can push a man only so far before he pushes back. Maybe something changes in his disposition once he has kids, something that makes him more prone to commit protective aggression and violence. Or maybe it's that my father was only twenty-one when the Charles Bronson movie *Death Wish* came out and put into his head the idea that vigilante violence is a valid answer to life's problems. I'm not sure. What I am sure of is that my father snapped.

His first step toward retaliation was to build what can only be described as a lair. Good old "wouldn't hurt a fly" Dad took a bunch of couch cushions and blankets and arranged them in a heap on our front porch. From the outside, it looked like a pile of garbage that was set on the porch to eventually be thrown out. Dad had decided to sit up all night, covered in these cushions and blankets, camouflaging himself, waiting for the teenage hooligans who had been causing him so much trouble. After five terrorized nights there was no reason to think they weren't coming back. They didn't realize that they had gone from predator to prey.

Of course, that night they no-showed. My father's hours of vigilance resulted merely in additional sleep deprivation.

"This is making things worse," my mother gently told him. "You can't fly off the handle like this."

The next night, he slept in his bed, embarrassed about his extreme behavior.

Needless to say, that night the teenage punks returned and kicked in the door.

My dad now felt like a fool, convinced that the teenagers were purposely toying with him. His anger returned and intensified. Insane or not, he told my mother he would be spending that night back in his rage nest, waiting for his chance to exact swift vengeance on his family's tormentors.

At about 2:30 A.M., my dad was woken from a light sleep by the laughter of the approaching youths. Slowly, quietly, he got up on his knees, making sure not to move so much that the kids would see him through the screens of the porch.

He heard one of them walking up the steps. One step, two steps, three steps.

Then, a crash.

Before the kid could rear back his foot to kick the door again, my father erupted from his pile of bedding bellowing a primal, rage-filled, Braveheart-battle scream. Immediately, the kids all screamed back in shock and terror.

In many ways, my father is not unlike a panda bear. First impressions of a panda are that it's nice, quiet, and adorable. My dad is the same way. But an angry panda bear is still a bear. It will fuck you up. No man emerges unscathed from a battle with a fucking panda. Cute or not, it will tear you apart instantly. As mentioned, my dad's six foot two and weighs in around 220 pounds. When in a good mood, he seems like a lovable goofball. A nice guy, as my friends have described him. When angry, he's something else entirely—he's an angry panda bear.

The kids, about four or five of them, spun around and took off. But instead of simply being content with his terrifying ambush, my father flew out the front door, landed on the sidewalk, screamed again, and took off after them. The kids left him in the dust—initially. But what they couldn't have known was that in high school my dad had played football. And his nickname was "the Dump Truck."

If a dump truck was sitting still, and someone asked you to outrun it once it started up, you could probably do so for the first hundred yards or so. It's big and clunky and takes a while to get going. But give it just a minute to gather some steam, and then see what happens.

These kids were being chased by a human, momentum-gathering Dump Truck. And that Dump Truck was being driven by the Angry Panda Bear.

The kids made a left and cut through the gravel parking lot of Colgate Park, but to their surprise and terror the Dump Truck was right on their asses. They sprinted toward the outfield of the park's baseball field in full panic. My father could see them, out in the open; they were like helpless gazelle loose on the plains. Sensing their fear, he sped up.

But the kids had an advantage. They had spent a lot more time in the park at night than my dad had. What they knew, and he didn't, was that each night the park's caretakers strung a chain across the end of the parking lot so that cars couldn't enter the park.

In the dark the knee-high chain was basically invisible, and my father ran straight into it. Serving the same function as a tripwire set up in the jungle by malicious Vietcong or surprisingly inventive Ewoks, it sent the big man sprawling into the field face-first.

It had recently rained, so when my father hit the ground he slid, face- and chest-down, ten feet out into the grass. There was a lot of mud on the field that night, and when he stood back up, he was covered head to toe in thick brown sludge. The kids, who must have been sure their freedom was at hand, could only stare dumbfounded as my father rose without missing a stride—his eyes and teeth now the only parts of him visible beneath the mud—and continued his pursuit.

Colgate Park's outfield goes uphill and is bordered by a large concrete wall. My father realized that in their panic, the kids were boxing themselves in against the wall. One by one they hit it, turned around, and saw he was still coming. When he got to them, they huddled next to each other, backs pinned against the concrete. They were terrified, and had every right to be. My father, covered in mud, was grinning like a lunatic and laughing with glee. His terrifying words didn't match this joyous mood.

He wheezed from the run while making eye contact with each of the kids.

"I'M GONNA COME BACK HERE TOMORROW NIGHT," he finally bellowed, "AND START CAVING IN SKULLS WITH A PIPE."

He then howled with laughter. He repeated the same sentence for three straight minutes, his hysterical laughter interrupted only by his rants and ravings about killing teenagers with a pipe.

When the cops arrived my father was initially pleased to see them, until they drew their guns on him. It didn't dawn on him that they might not be as concerned with disciplining scared teenagers as they were with securing the mud-covered madman joyously shouting about committing murder with a pipe.

My old man quickly realized the severity of the situation and wisely cooled down. He explained to the cops what had been happening—the property damage, his two young sons and re-covering wife, the multiple incidents of nighttime vandalism.

The cops didn't need to hear much. They were familiar with the park and the kids who loitered there. They told my dad to head home and turned their attention to the troublemakers.

The next morning there was a knock on our door. It was one of the punks from the night before. His father was with him, and the kid was holding a brand-new door. He apologized profusely, unable to mask the unadulterated fear that my father, even when not covered in mud, now produced deep within his soul.

The kid and his dad took down our severely beaten-up front door and installed the new one. The kid apologized again, and his dad assured my father there would be no further trouble. And for the five years we stayed in that house, there was none.

I've never personally seen my father as mad as that story re-counts. But I've often felt that mad myself. I suppose you could say that it's the part of his legacy that lives on in me. I'm not physically intimidating like my dad. Sadly, I inherited the tiny, malnutritioned-looking Irish stature of my mom's side of the family. I didn't stand a chance of playing high school football. I don't share my dad's interest in tap water, either, and since I have a woeful inability to grow facial hair, his moustache shall unfortunately die with him as well. But his anger—his mud-on-the-face, murder-in-the-eyes anger—is something that will live on in our bloodline forever.

My desire to tell embarrassing stories about our loved ones, meanwhile, is something I inherited from my mom. She's also the one who taught me that in some cases these stories can continue to grow well after the events that inspired them. Especially since it's best to leave out certain sensitive details until enough time has safely passed and everyone can look back and laugh about them.

For this story, that length of time was twenty-nine years.

It wasn't until Christmas Eve of 2009 when, during a special holiday retelling of the story by my mother, she added a line none of us had ever heard before.

"I was scared he was going to get arrested," she said, "*and that's why I called the cops on him.*"

My father froze, a decades-old anger roaring back to life in his eyes.

"You did what?" he asked. "You're the one who called the cops on me?"

"I thought you were gonna murder somebody," she calmly said. "And I'm sorry, but I didn't feel like raising two kids on my own."

Then we opened presents, like I imagine normal families do.

Pa

When I first started having panic attacks, or more accurately, when I finally started seeking treatment for them, my shrink told me I needed to find out if my family had a history of mental illness. That meant asking my mother to fill me in on any information she might have.

"Well . . . ," my mother said, shifting uncomfortably at our kitchen table.

"Ma, it's me, I don't care," I told her. "They just need to know."

"Let's see . . . on my side of the family, a bunch of people are on antidepressants," she said. "My dad never got treatment, but probably should have. And—"

"And what?" I said. She was clearly trying to find a way out of the conversation.

"Well, Pa was once in a mental hospital," she told me, her shoulders slumping.

It explained so much.

~~~

We moved to Alan Street when I was in kindergarten. Even though the new neighborhood was just a few short miles from our old house, the differences were like night and day. We were in a better school district. The area was cleaner and safer.

An added benefit—or, some would say, a severe drawback— was that the new neighborhood was full of members of my extended family.

My maternal grandparents lived three blocks away. Two blocks in the opposite direction were my mom's sister and her husband. Around the corner from us on Valley Way were my father's amazingly talkative sister Joan and three of my cousins. And just around the corner were my paternal grandparents, Grammy and Pa.

Living a stone's throw from our grandparents was magical for my brother and me. Suddenly we could say and do no wrong. Instead, these wonderful old people actually applauded our misbehavior. They thought it was cute and convinced our parents over and over again that we shouldn't be punished. My grandmother's contributions to my diet consisted primarily of butterscotch and ice cream sodas. Her definition of candy was pretty liberal, too.

"Grandma, can I have some candy?"

"Of course, Chris. Here's a spoon. There's sugar in that bowl."

And so the good times rolled, until my grandmother died of a stroke in 1987 and Pa responded by what can only be described as "freaking the fuck out."

As an adult, I would learn that Pa and Grammy's relationship was far more complex than it had seemed to me when I was a kid. According to my parents, Pa had been pretty dependent on Grammy for most of his adult life. During his middle-age years, anxiety about his work at Westinghouse led to a severe set of breakdowns, and that's what landed him in the Overbrook Mental Facility in Verona, New Jersey. He bounced back, but a few years later he underwent a botched operation, and afterward became even more nervous and fearful. This time, instead of entering a hospital, he clung to my grandma. Even to my young eyes, it was clear that he was scared to leave her side. He depended on her for almost everything. And she stood by him faithfully. With her help, he was able to live a pretty normal life. Of course, as a seven-year-old, I wasn't aware of any of this. I just knew that after my grandma died, Pa turned scary.

The transformation was quick and pronounced. Pa showed up at our front door every day, looking helpless. Once inside, after grunting hello, he'd sit on the couch in our basement watching sports. He remained silent for hours at a time. Gregg or I would bring him his dinner every night, and he'd mumble a few words of thanks and send us on our way. Each night when I'd head to bed, the sounds of the TV reaching my bedroom reminded me that he was still there. Each morning, he'd be gone.

Eventually, this got to be too much. My parents asked Pa to stay at his own house a few days a week so that Gregg and I could play in the basement and my mom could clean it. Pa was hurt, and took this suggestion as a request to never step foot in our house again. He retreated to his home and became even more reclusive. Gregg and I would visit him, until one night he pulled us aside.

"You shouldn't come here anymore," he said, grim and serious.

I looked at Gregg, who asked Pa, "Well, why not?"

Pa leaned in close to our faces.

"Because your grandmother's ghost haunts this house," he said, "and you don't want to make the ghost angry."

In hindsight, I realize he was simply depressed and wanted to be left alone—but at the time, his warnings of my grandma's ghost frightened me to my core, because I was a little kid and shit like that is scary. I dreaded the times my mother would send me to Pa's house to borrow a tool or bring him food. I'd stand on his steps, shaking, praying the ghost wouldn't get me. It would be nine years before I again stepped inside his house.

~~~

After my mother finished filling me in on my family's history of various mental difficulties, I felt exposed and uncomfortable.

"Mom," I asked her, "do you think I'm going to be okay?"

"Well," she answered. "Pa got better."

~~~

Pa emerged from his self-imposed isolation around 1992 a changed man. No one knew for sure what caused his rebirth, but something had happened inside that house that led him to a true revelation, in two parts: (1) He was old and going to die soon, and (2) he could therefore say and do whatever the fuck he wanted, anytime, anywhere.

One of my first experiences with the "new Pa" occurred while I was in sixth grade. I awoke early one Saturday to watch cartoons but was interrupted by furious knocking on our back door. I ran to open it, wearing only my underwear, and saw a frightened Pa frantically motioning for me to let him in. He leapt through the door before I even had it completely open, knocking me backward. His rambling was nonstop except for quick gasps for breath, punctuated by wild gestures toward the yard. I looked out the window and saw a skunk sitting on our lawn, completely motionless.

"Oh well, time to call animal control," my mom said, picking up the phone.

Pa reached over and put the phone back onto the receiver.

"Oh to hell with that, get me a broom," he replied in his trademark ornery style. "I'm going to kill it." We all turned and stared at him in disbelief.

"What?" I asked.

"There's a trick to killing a skunk," he said. He put his hand on my shoulder and looked me in the eye. "You take a stick and bash it right on the tip of its nose. They have soft bones. Hit them in the right spot and their skulls cave in. You crush their brains."

"No!" I shouted, locking eyes with Pa and shaking my head. I looked to my parents and grabbed at my hair in disbelief. "Are you just going to let him kill it?"

"Ahh to hell with you," Pa shouted. "Get me the goddamned broom!" I looked back to my father, who nodded at me. I went and got the broom.

Pa was in his seventies, but when he got that broom in his hand he became as agile as a collegiate wrestler. He leapt off the porch, wielding the broom like a Filipino eskrima stick. He inched closer to the skunk and raised the broomstick in the air, allowing it to hover above the unsuspecting beast. With deadly precision, he brought it down on the animal's nose. The poor creature collapsed onto its side. I screamed.

Pa picked the skunk up and walked toward me. In my panic I could only shout the word "No," over and over again. Pa grinned and tossed the animal at me. I had no choice but to catch it.

At which point I realized it was dead and stuffed, albeit ultra-realistic.

Pa, it turned out, had been up since six in the morning, lurking in our yard. He was waiting for any signs that I was awake
inside the house, for the sole purpose of seeing my reaction
when he pretended to murder an animal in front of me.

~~~

"Really?" I asked my mom. "He got better? Because he seemed
pretty out there."

My mom laughed as she sipped her tea.

~~~

Pa refused to give up his Buick, though he had no right driving
at his age. Besides swerving like a blacked-out drunk, he drove
so slowly that the neighborhood kids would race his car, on
foot, up our hill. We always won.

My father was filled with anxiety whenever he saw his dad
behind the wheel. Gardening has always been one of the few activities that clears my dad's mind in times of stress. During my
childhood he would often come home from work brooding and
quiet, only to head into our yard to tend to his tomato plants.
After an hour or so, he'd emerge, covered in dirt but visibly
more relaxed. Gardening is to my father what weird hippie yoga
is to other people. For my father, Pa's driving was definitely a
cause for gardening.

One day, a kickball game I was embroiled in was interrupted
when Pa's car turned the corner and headed up the block. We
cleared the way so he could pass. There was no need. Pa plowed
directly into the back of a brand-new Jeep that was parked in
front of the Tylers' house. Audrey Tyler's boyfriend flew out
the door.

"My car! Shit!" he shouted, dismayed at the destruction wrought to his taillights.

"It's okay," Pa shouted from his window. "I'm Kenny's father!" He then pointed in the direction of my dad, who'd been peacefully tending the flowers on our front lawn. Pa waved to my dad and drove away, leaving my father—who was clearly mortified, on his knees and holding gardening tools—alone to deal with the situation. I don't think my father ever found as much peace in gardening after that day.

~~~

"You were too young to really remember him before Grammy died," my mom explained. "I knew him when she was alive, and saw how hard it hit him."

I looked up at my mom, who smiled.

"I think Pa was weird," she continued. "But weird was better than sad."

~~~

For Pa's eightieth birthday, our family gathered for a party at my uncle's house. It was rare for some members on my father's side of the family to admit each other's existence, let alone be in one place together. I was fifteen, and it was the first time in my life that I remember everyone acting polite and cordial to each other. Aunt Joan wasn't talking as much as usual, which is to say she was only talking constantly. My one uncle didn't tell his joke about Hitler being his favorite American. All seemed strangely right.

But no one was speaking to my brother. I would touch base with him, then go off to catch up with someone else, only to see him standing alone in a corner, looking confused, or eating chips while everyone ignored him. Gregg was as baffled as I was.

"Dude, did you say something to piss everyone off?" I asked.

"Chris, I know I sometimes say weird shit," he said, "but I swear to God, I have no idea why nobody's talking to me."

Fearing that his social leprosy might rub off on me, I left him standing next to a cooler of my Aunt Karen's famous homemade lemonade and got back to the party.

Eventually, Gregg was approached by Kathy, one of my female cousins (the sassy one in her early thirties who lived in Manhattan, making her "open-minded").

"You know, Gregory, I'm fine with whatever you choose," Kathy told him.

"Uh . . . okay, thanks," Gregg replied.

"Not everyone here will support your decision," she continued, "but I respect it. I may not *understand* it, but I respect that it's how you want to live. And you're going off to college next year, so now's the time to figure it all out."

"Umm . . . okay?" Gregg managed to squeak out.

I walked back over to Gregg.

"They think I'm gay," he said.

I scanned the yard and saw many raised eyebrows thrown our way. Suspicions were being tossed toward Gregg with the subtlety of an early '90s Jim Carrey movie.

"Why do they think that?" I asked. True, my brother was shy, and never had a girlfriend to bring around, but that was rooted in his status as a skinny weirdo who was obsessed with pro wrestling and geography, not in any disinterest in ladies.

Gregg stared across the yard. Pa was seated in a folding chair, looking directly at us. Our grandfather laughed wildly and slapped his knee in obvious delight.

"I'm pretty sure," Gregg sighed, "that Pa told everyone I'm gay."

As the evening wore on, people began quietly asking me how I felt about my brother's sexual awakening.

"Well, the thing is," I told one second cousin, "he's not gay. I'm not really sure how that rumor started, but it's not true."

"Huh," my cousin grunted, his Jersey mullet catching the wind. "I don't know. . . ."

My brother and Pa didn't talk for years after that. It was only after Pa's death that I got Gregg to admit that our grandfather's prank was fucking hilarious.

~~~

"He was crazy," I told my mother. "But at least he was crazy in a good way."

"Yeah," she said. "It's not so bad. You just have to figure out how to be crazy in a good way, too."

~~~

My greatest moment with Pa came when I was a sophomore in high school. It was that amazing time of year on the East Coast, those three or four days during fall when a cool breeze is already blowing but the sun is still shining, and the leaves have just about fully changed but none have fallen.

I was on the phone in my bedroom, kicking it to a husky freshman named Melissa (who would inevitably turn me down), when I smelled a smoky odor wafting in through my second-floor window. I stuck my head outside and looked around the neighborhood.

All seemed normal. In the middle of the street, Jerry Hubert was competing with Matt Kehoe and Nick Scagliozzi in a fierce game of wiffle ball. In the background, I could see Pa doing a strange dance in his backyard. Par for the course.

I continued flirting with the chunky apple of my eye. The smoky smell worsened, but I was in the zone, really working a good sophomore-in-high-school game, and didn't pay it any attention until my mom charged up the stairs.

"Chris! Chris! *Pa's lawn is on fire!*" she screamed.

I looked out the window again to see that Pa's dancing had taken a turn for the worse. The kids had stopped playing wiffle ball and were gathered near his fence.

"Go!" my mom said. "You have to help him!"

I couldn't figure out what my mother meant. His lawn was on fire? That concept made, and still makes, very little sense to me.

"Is everything okay?" I heard Melissa's distant voice ask. I brought the handset back to my ear and tried to sound as heroic as possible.

"I'll call you back," I said in a half-whisper. "I've got to go save my grandpa." My voice didn't sound even vaguely heroic, as it still hadn't changed by the age of fifteen.

I flew down the steps and charged out the door. I headed straight across Mrs. Burns's lawn and vaulted over Pa's rusted chain-link fence in one leap.

Foot-high licks of flame were rising out of my grandfather's grass. It had been a hot summer and much of the yard was dead and browned. Pa was trying to stamp the flames away. I needed to get him out of there.

"Pa, come on!" I shouted. "We gotta call the fire department."

He looked me dead in the eye and replied, "Fuck you."

My jaw dropped. *Did my grandfather just say fuck me?* I looked at him, breathing heavily, staring me down. He had. He had definitely said fuck me.

"I can handle this," he continued, before turning around and stamping his foot into a three-foot-wide, one-foot-high swath of fire.

I glared at the old man.

"You gonna let him talk to you like that?" one of the neighborhood kids shouted from beyond the fence. I couldn't see which kid yelled it as there was now a wall of smoke rising between us. My anger was quickly replaced by fear.

Pa's lawn was *shooting fire at us*, and his stomping of the flames was only spreading fire to other patches of grass. Even worse, because Pa had developed kidney problems, the nerves in his feet were deadened. In horror, I watched as his trademark brown loafers caught flame as he brought them down into the inferno. The motion of raising his foot blew the flames out, at which point he'd stomp down again, igniting his shoe once more. Because he had no feeling in his feet he had no idea this was happening.

The flames reached the edge of his property and spread to bushes that had been placed there by landscapers who had evidently also sprayed them down with heavily flammable insecticides. One by one, the shrubs turned into six-foot-tall spires of flame. It was like being in the first circle of hell, or on the set of a Mexican game show. I shouted to the neighborhood kids to get Mrs. Burns out of her house before it caught fire.

The old man refused to leave. He'd decided that if his house was going to burn, he was going down with the ship. I had to put out the fire, and needed to find the tools to do so. Grandma's ghost or not, I was going to have to go inside Pa's house.

I ran through Pa's back doorway and up the steps into the kitchen, where I froze in my tracks. It had been so long since I'd seen the place that I didn't even remember the layout. There was something tomblike and sealed off from time about the room that gave me the creeps. I took a deep breath that stung in my chest. I didn't know if it was from smoke inhalation or the lingering fear that my grandmother's disembodied form was about to descend upon me.

I was walking through a bizarre time capsule of my own childhood. Some cardboard blocks painted to look like bricks lay scattered on the back porch, clearly untouched since the last time my brother and I had played with them. A clock I'd painted and given to my grandma when I was four hung above the kitchen table, exactly where she'd placed it the day I gave it to her. The hands were frozen in place.

My fear was replaced with profound sadness. Pa had been sitting in this house for years, just thinking about my grandma. He didn't change anything about his life or his surroundings. He'd shared this home with his wife for over fifty years. She died. Some time later—who knows when?—that clock died. And clearly Pa spent the last portion of his life doing little more than sitting inside his house waiting to die as well.

An occasional car crash here. A skunk and/or homosexuality-driven prank there. They were very minor distractions at the end of a very long life. Nothing more.

The only thing that could be more depressing would be letting my grandpa die in a fire. I had to find a way to help him.

I ran to the basement looking for a washbasin or bucket—nothing. I sprinted back to the kitchen. Panic was setting in as I laid my eyes on my only hope to save the day.

Look, it's not like I thought using a teapot to put out a raging fire was a great idea. It's just that during a crisis, you've got to do *something*. So I filled Pa's teapot to its brim—a whopping three to four cups' worth of water. I ran back into the yard and dumped the water as if I was pouring tea—through the spout part. This

produced a round of applause and laughter from the neighborhood kids standing on the other side of the fence, finding their
afternoon entertainment in the prospect that I might be burned
alive before their eyes. I ran back in and refilled the teapot, then
ran back out, only to see Pa's next-door neighbor spraying down
the lawn with his hose.

I breathed a huge sigh of relief. Frazzled and exhausted, I
walked over to Pa and placed my hand on the old man's back.
He was surely terrified by this whole thing, but I had come to
his aid. I realized that my patting his back was the most physical
contact, and the most intimate moment, we'd shared in almost
a decade. I felt a profound sense of closeness with my grandfather, and I vowed that this strange, awful experience would
serve as the impetus for my taking better care of the guy, being
there for him more often.

He looked at me with what I thought was pride in his eyes. I
figured he was experiencing the same sentiments. Then he spoke
and brought me back down to Earth.

"This is all your fault!" he shouted, scorn filling his voice.

"What? How could this possibly be my fault?" I asked.

"I asked you to mow my lawn," he shot back. "You didn't, so I
just lit it on fire!"

For the record, he had never asked me anything of the sort.

~~~

Pa died in 2003. His skunk was the only thing I asked to inherit.
I still have it.

The fact is, Pa represents some of the genetic material that
contributed to my very existence. It's a frightening thought, but
one that fills me with a great amount of hope as well.

One day, I'll be old. Everyone will have died or left me, and I will be alone. Maybe depression will have a hold on me, or my grasp on reality will have slipped. I will sense that my day of reckoning is at hand, and I will undoubtedly be scared.

When that day comes, I pray that I will find strength. Not the strength to endure, and not the strength to come to grips with the life I've led and the mistakes I've made. I know myself well enough to know that such strength will be beyond me to summon.

Instead, I pray for the strength to reach for the stuffed skunk that is my grandfather's legacy. For the strength to live my final days as he did—distracting myself from my ultimate fate with weirdness and fun.

I pray for the strength during my final days to strike the match that will set my whole world on fire, as my grandfather did before me.

Koozo

Koozo.

In my neighborhood, it was a name that could only be spoken in whispers.*

I first met the man known as Koozo when he climbed out of a sewer pipe at the bottom of my street wearing mesh shorts and no underwear. I had been playing kickball with a few other kids when we saw him emerge from the depths to approach us.

"Hey, I'm Koozo," he said, wild-eyed and grinning.

"Do you know we can see your wiener?" my brother asked. No sense in beating around the bush when it comes to something as prominent as an exposed phallus.

"Yeah," Koozo answered, grinning. "Yeah, I do know that."

Koozo, or Jack Koozling, grew up around the block from me, on Mississippi Avenue. I spent the better part of my childhood living in the grip of a curious combination of fascination and fear that he inspired.

---

*This line was stolen from my brother, who feared Koozo even more than I did.

27

For the entire time I knew him, no one was sure how old Koozo was. He was either a very burly teenager or an under-developed young man—it was hard to tell. Asking Koozo about his age revealed nothing. Like most conversations with Koozo, it only made clear that his plane of reality was a few steps away from ours.

"Koozo, man," one might nonchalantly say, "how old are you turning this year?"

"Ha," Koozo would respond. "I'm as old as the hills, man. I've always existed. *And I always will.*"

This mystery was further compounded by Koozo's propensity for showing up to play with us preteen kids driving a car. It meant either that Koozo was at least seventeen—the legal driving age in New Jersey and thus far older than the kids he played with regularly—or that he had stolen a car. Neither option would have surprised anyone who knew him.

While Koozo preferred to keep many things about himself am-biguous, one thing he made absolutely clear was his fondness for another set of wheels more prized than even the car he "owned": his infamous moped. It's been twenty years since I first met Koozo. I've moved on, physically and emotionally, from that place and time. I haven't lived in the old neighborhood for over a decade. But I guarantee that if I ran into anyone originally from that part of town and brought up Koozo, they could instantly impersonate the sound of his moped. That unmistakable sound, like a lawn-mower on steroids, was burned into the brains of anyone who grew up in my pocket of West Orange, New Jersey, during the '80s. The first time I saw the moped was one morning when I looked out my window to see Koozo doing donuts on our front lawn.

A moped is a motorized bike that can be run either by engine or by pedaling, making it the ideal mode of transportation for lunatics. Pedaling allowed Koozo to silently sneak up on unsuspecting prey. My street was a dead end on a hill. Like all successful predators, Koozo recognized an ideal hunting ground when he saw one. There were countless times when my group of friends would be playing some innocent game in the street as night fell. When darkness settled in around us, the peace of our suburban existence would be thrown into chaos when a lone headlight blinked on at the top of the hill. This would be followed by the unmistakable sound of Koozo's moped roaring to life. Invariably, it would take Koozo a few attempts to get the motor running—it was in these few precious seconds that we learned to act, to run, to hide. It was through the terror of these repeated experiences that I first became familiar with the "fight or flight" mentality. Anyone who played on my street understood that concept from a young age. And each and every one of us chose flight, categorically.

"Koozo!" we'd all shout while fleeing for our lives. Shouting the word "Koozo" was the most any of us ever did to look out for our friends. "Koozo" was like our *shalom* or *aloha*—it had many meanings. The word referred to a man and simultaneously to a mythology surrounding him; it was also synonymous with the word "run."

Teaming up and fighting back against the maniacal manchild's attack were options never considered. Running was the only priority when Koozo struck. The growls of the engine sliced through the peace of the night as he charged toward us at top speed, around thirty miles per hour. Often, Koozo would brandish a thorn branch, which he would lash out at us as he passed, like a Roman piloting a chariot and swinging a whip. I also once saw him riding his moped with a lawn-pruning tool some eight feet in length, balanced on the handlebars like a medieval lancing joust. Koozo was one of those rare childhood characters who wasn't merely posturing—we figured that he aimed to hurt us, and if we stood around, he certainly would have.

Just a few years ago I was talking with my mother about how, with age, perspective tends to change.

"Take someone like Koozo," I said. "To us, he was the most frightening person ever. To you guys, the grown-ups, he was probably just some weird hyperactive kid."

"Oh no," my mother answered. "I thought he was a maniac."

I looked at her in complete shock.

"I mean, just from the little glimpses I got," she said. "Koozo was scary."

Koozo's strategy in capturing us was not unlike that of a large game cat as it approaches herd animals—isolate the slow, sick, or weak and allow the others to scatter. For example, Dave Kearns, one of the elder members of the fourteen-child-strong Kearns family, had notoriously bad knees. During one of Koozo's attacks I watched as the deranged crackpot drove straight toward us, sending each kid looking for hiding places of any available sort. Koozo masterfully noticed that Dave's sprint was a half-step slower than most and targeted him instantly. Koozo sped up, popped a wheelie, and slammed into Dave from behind, sending the boy hurtling head-first into a bush. We all watched in horror from our hiding places. Koozo laughed maniacally, circling Dave, who was trapped helplessly inside a piece of shrubbery on the Kostyak family's front lawn. It was clear to us that Koozo wanted others to come forward to help Dave, so he could pick them off one by one. The headlight of the moped scanned other bushes for preteen prey. And though from our hiding places the light blinded us, we could hear him out there, laughing like the maniac that he was.

Needless to say, none of us stepped out to help Dave.

The kids in my neighborhood played a game called "Caughtie," a team-based and slightly more violent version of hide-and-seek. Koozo often joined in wearing an outfit that could have belonged to a covert operative for the CIA being sent deep into the jungle. This typically consisted of an all-black sweat suit, black combat boots, a black wool hat (even in the middle of summer), and, best of all, camouflage face paint.

It was quickly learned that if we wanted the game to be any fun at all, Koozo's team *never hid first.* Because Koozo was *impossible to find.* He hid in trees. In sewers. On rooftops. In places we obviously never even knew about, because, again, we could never find him. If Koozo's team hid first, the game would be reduced to a group of bored kids wandering around looking for him in quiet frustration. And in the rare event someone did manage to catch a fleeting glimpse of Koozo, there was no chance in hell they could get close enough to him to tag him. Not only was he stronger and faster than the rest of us, he seemed mentally unstable in a way that made him willing to go to any lengths to avoid capture.

I once saw Koozo being chased by a few kids who noticed him moving from one hiding spot to another. A crowd quickly grew, roused by the thought that this was their chance to catch the elusive Koozo—an act that, if accomplished, would cement their status as neighborhood legends. Koozo sprinted to a telephone pole and spun around with his back to it. In that moment, the faintest glimmer of fear flashed in the eyes of the Mighty Koozo. As the opposing team gathered, Koozo looked from side to side, but there was no escape. Or so we thought. There were a few hard-and-fast rules in our neighborhood: you didn't go past Colgate Park at night, you never walked down the block of Elm Street where Gay George lives, and under no circumstances did you underestimate Koozo.

"It's over, Koozo!" one of the kids shouted as Koozo frantically looked for an escape.

"I can't believe it," I said to my brother as we both watched.

"Shut up," he said. "I want to see this." His desire to keep the experience unsullied by my talking was justified. We were watching history unfold.

Then, to the surprise of everyone watching, Koozo turned and faced the pole. The rival team continued to approach, ready to claim their glory. But at the last possible moment victory was snatched from their hands when Koozo hugged the telephone pole and shimmied halfway up its length. The kids gathered at its base. Koozo may have found a short-term solution, but he had to come down sometime. All they had to do was wait.

Koozo had other plans. He had no intention of coming down. Climbing with a dexterity seen exclusively in ninjas and chimpanzees, Koozo continued up the pole. What happened next can only be attributed to the wild, gutsy bravado of a kid willing to put his life on the line for a simple game.

From his perch on the pole Koozo slowly stepped out onto the electrical wire that ran from telephone pole to telephone pole and proceeded to walk across it as if on a circus tightrope, gripping the wire above his head for balance. Mouths agape, all the kids stopped chasing him to watch, expecting Koozo to be electrocuted, fall to his death, or suffer some terrible combination of both. When he got to the next pole, he slid back down to the ground and took off into the wild. No one bothered chasing after him.

"God damn Koozo," Gregg finally said, shaking his head as we walked away.

"God damn Koozo," I echoed.

The game ended like all Caughtie games with Koozo did: eventually, after the sun had gone down, everyone got bored

and wandered home, leaving Koozo sitting in whatever unde-
tectable hiding spot he had found for himself.

~~~

My mother's best friend was a special-education teacher in our
town. This meant she dealt with the emotionally disturbed—of
which some of us may have considered Koozo a prime example.
Legend had it Koozo was so bad that before graduating elementary
school he had already done turns in every local public school and
been banned from entering them. For a while my mother's friend
had to travel to Koozo's home at night to tutor him personally. The
first time she attempted this, the story went, she arrived on his
front porch and rang the doorbell. No one answered. Lights were
on and she could clearly make out the sounds of a television coming from inside, so she knew people were home. She figured Koozo
was just ignoring her, hiding out in hopes of dodging schoolwork.
She had experienced worse situations and kept ringing the bell.

"I mean, I've seen it all, but . . . ," I overheard her say as she
told my mother the story years ago at our kitchen table. "You
shouldn't let your kids around him. I mean, I've never seen anything like that, before or since."

After about ten minutes, the door finally opened. In the background, she could see Koozo's father asleep on a couch. Koozo
answered the door himself. He was wearing a T-shirt, but was
otherwise nude. In his hand he was holding a roll of paper towels.

It was on fire.

~~~

We had ample reason to believe Koozo's pyromania didn't stop
at setting household cleaning supplies aflame in the buff. One

night, Koozo showed up on my street with a bag of fireworks. Fireworks, though illegal, were a hot commodity in my neighborhood. Rory Kearns was well known for his love of M-80s, which he used to put on public demonstrations that involved blowing up cinder blocks. Andy Connor, a grimy, gap-toothed bully who lived on Calvin Terrace, was known to employ fireworks as one of his many intimidation tactics, threatening to burn kids with their sparks. Fireworks were one of the things that separated the men from the boys, the weapon of choice for true badasses in our corner of the world.

On this particular night, Koozo showed up and trumped everyone.

"They're called nigger chasers," Koozo told us as he held out a handful of cheaply made explosives. This blunt language was shocking, even from a guy who seemed as unhinged as Koozo did.

"Ah, they just look like bottle rockets," someone chimed in from the back of the crowd that had gathered around Koozo. "Who cares?"

"They're not bottle rockets," Koozo snapped. "They're nigger chasers. You see that eye on the side?" He pointed to a drawing that looked vaguely like the logo for CBS broadcasting.

"Yeah. What about it?" someone indignantly asked.

"That eye looks for anything dark," Koozo growled. "And it's like a heat-seeking missile that goes after anything black it comes across."

I remember shifting uncomfortably, and thinking to myself, *This is fucked up, even for our neighborhood.*

But before I could completely formulate that thought, someone decided to challenge Koozo's claims of the darkness-chasing qualities of his racist fireworks. A faceless member of the crowd shouted out the one contentious phrase certain to cause trouble among any self-respecting group of preteen males.

"Prove it."

Everyone "oohed" at the prospect of Koozo being challenged. Koozo got angry. He squinted his eyes and puffed out his chest. He told everyone to back up.

"Let's see . . . let's see . . . ," he said quietly, looking for a worthy target. His eyes locked onto my house. "There! Mr. Gethard's wearing a black shirt."

Everyone, myself included, turned to see my father gardening on our front lawn. Apparently, the mental effects of my grandfather's car crash had finally worn off and my dad was again finding peace in helping some of Mother Nature's creatures grow.

"Now wait a second," I said. "Don't even—"

I was cut off by the taunts of the kids I was standing among. Koozo threw a pile of fireworks onto the ground, wiped the sweat from his palms by rubbing them across his dingy shorts, and removed a lighter from his pocket. He went down to one knee in front of the fireworks, and took on the serious facial expressions and body language of a World War II infantryman about to fire mortar shells at the enemy.

"Koozo, man," I said, "it's my dad."

My protests fell on deaf ears. Everyone ignored me as the anticipation of Koozo's airborne attack on my father grew. I glanced over to Gregg, who shrugged his shoulders. There was nothing we could do to stop it. We could only wait to see how it turned out.

Koozo lit the first firecracker and pointed it toward my dad. It shrieked through the night, a trail of light marking its path as it headed straight for the old man, only to get caught up in the branches of a small nearby tree. It exploded in a shower of sparks.

My dad flipped onto his back, his eyes wide in terror. He raised the hand-sized pitchfork he had been working with, waving it defensively at no one. Just then, another firework exploded above his shoulder, causing him to spin wildly, searching the horizon for his assailant. His eyes spotted Koozo as the maniacal boy/man leaned down to light yet another missile. My dad twisted onto his stomach and crawled down the hill that marked the edge of our property. As quickly as he could, he leapt behind the corner of our house.

When he stuck his head out moments later, another firecracker careened past him, exploding against the wall of the Scagliozzis' home next door. My dad used this as his opportunity to flee. He vaulted over the low-lying bush that ran along the walkway to our front door. He leapt up all three stairs and flung open the door, falling forward into our porch just as another firework whipped past him, narrowly missing his feet as he finally escaped into the safety of our home. Moments later, Koozo fired off one last rocket for good measure, though my father was long gone. It exploded in front of our house, and was followed by an eerie silence and the smell of gunpowder.

"See?" Koozo said with no small amount of glee in his voice. "Black shirt. Chased him that whole time. Nigger chasers."

~~~

As years passed, Koozo appeared less and less frequently. My final encounter with him occurred when I was almost done with high school. It had been a good three years since I'd seen hide or hair of him.

One afternoon, my brother and I were fiddling around with a police scanner (don't ask why—the answer is that we're losers and dorks) when we picked up someone broadcasting on a CB, inviting truckers to congregate at Our Lady of Lourdes church. This was our church, only three short blocks from our home. We snuck down to Lourdes to see what was going on. There were four or five full-blown eighteen-wheelers circled in the parking lot. In the middle of this ring of big rigs, sitting on the hood of his car, was Koozo, grinning and gesticulating wildly as he shouted to the truckers in their cabs. From our distance we couldn't hear what he was saying, and, creeped out by the whole scene, we didn't stick around long enough to figure out what his intentions were in summoning them.

Years later, my brother Gregg and I were talking about how we grew up.

"Dude," I said, "if you had to describe Koozo in three words, what would they be?"

My brother answered without thinking twice.

"Greaseball," he said. "Caughtie. CB radio advocate."

I was so surprised that he didn't say "moped."

After his afternoon trucker rendezvous, we never heard from Koozo again. I never saw Koozo grow up or knew him as an adult, and I'm glad I never did. In my mind, he still exists as he was— the scourge of the sewers and the terror of the treetops. I'd like to believe that out there in some peaceful suburban neighborhood he's running a terrified child over with a moped right now.

PS: There is a neighborhood secret that I am one of only a handful of people to know. I feared Koozo immensely at certain times in my childhood and never had the guts to come forward when I should have. Maybe it's too late to make amends now— I'm not sure. But a person's got to try, even fifteen years after the fact, I guess. So Mike Tenkman, if you're reading this, it was Koozo who stole and killed your leopard gecko.

My First Kiss

Her name was Samantha. Like most of the girls who spoke to me during high school, she was in the marching band. She played piccolo, meaning she had more rhythm than she did self-esteem. As an extension of these issues, she somehow managed to be both bulimic and chubby at the same exact time. And for some undefined reason, she constantly smelled of birch beer.

Needless to say, I was in love.

I sat directly behind Samantha in Ms. Flynn's sophomore English class. We didn't talk much, until the day I almost vomited directly on her face.

English was the first class of the day, and I had a bad habit of having to use the bathroom just as class was starting. I couldn't help it. My digestive tract was and is notoriously unstable. I interrupted class dozens of times before Ms. Flynn, who on most days was so nice and understanding it actually seemed sinister, put her foot down. She informed me that I would no longer be allowed to leave her class to use the restroom. I respected her enough to grin, bear it, and wait to use the restroom until after class.

While I understood Ms. Flynn's point of view, I knew in my heart that human biology stops for no English teacher. I respected her wishes and stopped asking for the hall pass, but understood deep down that the stage had been set for disaster.

"Ms. Flynn," I said one morning, almost a month after she had handed down her edict, "I really need to use the bathroom."

"Chris," she said, "I'm sorry. But I can't. We talked about this."

Unfortunately, she didn't realize that on this particular day I didn't have to "use the bathroom" at all—I had to throw up. Violently. And more importantly, immediately.

I raised my hand again, praying she would see the terror in my eyes.

"Chris, you can't go," she said.

"But—"

"No!" she said, glaring at me. "I said no, and I meant it." I had been put in my place, publicly. Stifled giggles filled the room. I had no choice but to tough it out.

No one wants to be the kid who gets yelled at for taking too many shits, I reminded myself through gritted teeth. *No one.*

My resolve lasted less than a minute. After a few seconds, I felt it: a wave of vomit suddenly rising from the depths of my stomach. At that moment, as my cheeks quickly ballooned with bile, Samantha spun around. Accompanying the rising tide of puke was a noise that every kid recognizes as the unmistakable prelude to throwing up. But Samantha, with her self-inflicted bouts of vomiting, was especially attuned to the sound and knew better than anyone exactly what it entailed. Her eyes widened. Somehow I managed to hold the steaming liquid inside my mouth. We made direct eye contact, and despite my own panic, I tried to convey that everything was going to be fine.

When you are fifteen, shy, and strange, you develop an acute awareness of the reactions of everyone around you to *you*, particularly of those you have a crush on. It is thanks to this that I will never forget the look on Samantha's face. I have never seen a woman react to me with as much disgust as Samantha did when she realized I was seconds from spewing hot stomach acid all over her cute, slightly pudgy face. It's strange, but I think the vomit filling my cheeks actually helped my confidence with women in the long term. I've found a certain strength in being absolutely sure I will never leave a worse impression on a woman than I did that morning as I loomed over my crush with puke ready to fly.

With cheeks full of throw-up, I calmly walked to the front of the room, made eye contact with Ms. Flynn, and yarfed the contents of my stomach into the garbage can.

No one even laughed—a surefire sign that something in a high school environment has gone from odd to fucked up. Ms. Flynn stood frozen in the center of the room, the chalk she had been writing with now resting in her trembling hand.

I wiped my sleeve against my vomit-covered chin.

"*Now* do you want to let me go to the bathroom?" I defiantly asked before strutting out of the room—without a hall pass. At that point it was easily the coolest thing I'd ever done.

Two things happened as a result of that incident. The first was that Ms. Flynn felt horrible, and for the rest of the year let me use the bathroom whenever I asked.

The second was that Samantha thought I was somehow cool for nearly vomiting on her face and then mouthing off to a teacher. Maybe it made me seem rebellious. Maybe she'd been waiting for a big-headed nerd with a dark side to come into her life. Or maybe seeing me vomit made her attracted to someone within whom she saw herself. All I know is that the incident made her oddly fascinated with me.

Shortly before the end of that year, fueled by my newfound vomit-driven confidence, I decided to put all of my cards on the table.

"Samantha," I told her one evening over the telephone, "I have to tell you something."

"Oh no," she said. "Do you like me or something?"

This was not the ideal response, to say the least.

Samantha let me down gently. I knew it was coming. While I'd been busy playing "Magic: The Gathering," she'd been actually dating. She routinely told me stories about how she spent her summers at the Jersey shore, which I imagined for any girl meant drinking vodka hidden in water bottles and hooking up with older dudes. As far as my imagination was concerned, she may as well have been regaling me with tales of her performing oral sex for the first (and second through eleventh) time(s) underneath the boardwalk.

Regardless of how much of it was actually true, rather than feeling jealous I found myself wanting to save Samantha from this wild-child lifestyle. I wanted to give her a sense of stability, the chance to build a relationship not out of boardwalk-driven hysteria but out of our mutual respect and devotion to each other.

Also, I wanted in on that blowjob stuff.

Samantha and I continued to talk on the phone, at least once a day. But we both knew it would soon be coming to an end—I was set to attend a three-week-long summer school debate program at Georgetown University. In my mind, this only further illustrated our differences. I was into talking heatedly about political issues. I assumed she was into getting drunk and kissing wieners underneath a series of wooden planks. It was never going to work.

Or so I thought. The night before I left, Samantha gave me a tearful phone call.

"Why do you have to go?" she asked through sobs. "I'm going to miss you."

"I'm going to miss you, too," I said. "But I am going to learn so much about debating. And that is definitely going to serve me well in the future."

It has not.

"But . . . ," she wept. "I'm in love with you."

"You're . . . what?"

We spent the rest of that night on the phone, crying, expressing to each other how happy we were that we had found love, with all the histrionics and hyperbole two teenagers could summon. Finally, someone felt the same way about me as I felt about her. We promised to stay true to each other while I was away.

"Be safe down there," she said. I'm not sure what dangers she thought I would encounter during a three-week program full of teenaged kids who liked to debate political hot-button issues. "When you come back, I'll be waiting."

"Okay," I said. "I promise, I'll be careful."

"Chris," she said. "I'm your girlfriend, okay?"

"Yeah," I whispered. "You're my girlfriend. That's okay."

Then, in the morning, I left.

That night, immediately after arriving, I bought a calling card and dialed Samantha. We talked late into the evening, and she told me that when I got home, we were hanging out the first night.

"And when we do," she told me, "it's going to be fun, for both of us."

"You mean like . . . ," I stammered.

"Yeah," she said. "That."

"Like we're gonna make out and stuff?" I said, smooth as always.

"Yeah. I keep saying yeah," she said, getting annoyed.

"Cool," I said. "That's so cool." I said my good-byes and hung up the phone, sensing that my awkwardness was ruining the conversation.

My floor of guys, whom I had just met that day, were psyched for me. Every one of them had more experience with girls than me, and enjoyed telling me all of their sordid tales of hooking up, passing it off as advice. I went to bed that night as happy as I had ever been, even though it had just been made explicitly clear that I was the least sexually experienced guy in a group of high school debate enthusiasts.

The next morning, I woke up still on cloud nine. I hopped out of bed, grabbed a towel, and headed down the hall to the communal shower in my underwear.

I opened the bathroom door, and inside was a Turkish guy named Ali. He was a Republican and, from what I remember, a fierce debater. But as he turned to face me I realized even then that I wouldn't remember Ali for his political leanings. What I would remember Ali for were his pubes. A full, jet-black bush that would forever burn itself into my memory. The kind that I now understand only a Turk can have at the age of fifteen.

I turned and headed straight back to my room, the spring noticeably absent from my step. I sat on my bed and felt like I had to shit, which is the number one indicator that I am experiencing severe anxiety. I got under my covers and proceeded to cry.

For about a year, I'd experienced a sneaking suspicion that I was drifting behind the pack, but I had no idea how thoroughly I'd been left behind. My school didn't make kids shower after gym. Everyone just went to their individual corner of the locker room and quickly changed. Most days, I put in so little effort in gym that I didn't sweat at all, so I generally didn't even have a need to remove my underwear. A few guys did get nude in the locker room, but they were mostly jocks who liked to do homo-erotic things as an excuse to say something homophobic. I didn't spend any time checking out their pubes.

And no one could have checked out mine. Because I had none.

For the rest of my three weeks at Georgetown, I participated in three separate rituals. First, I woke up every morning hours before any of my classes so that I could shower in an environ-ment where I was sure no one would see my weird, smooth, hair-less pubic mound. After classes and dinner, I called Samantha, my second ritual of the day. It was an over-the-phone love affair, easily (and sadly) the farthest I'd gotten with a girl.

My third ritual commenced at bedtime. Each night, I got un-der my covers, lifted my penis, and furiously examined the base of my shaft for any signs of pube growth.

I was furious at my dick. And instead of suffering quietly, I let it know.

"Why do you want to ruin this for me?" I asked pointedly. If anything in this world understood my affections for Samantha it should have been my penis. After all, it had been a sympa-thetic and willing participant in all of my many filthy fantasies about her.

Late one night my frustration reached a boiling point. "Grow!" I shouted at my pitiful, bald privates. "Grow! Grow! Grow!"

Moments later there was a knock at my door. I threw on a towel and answered it. It was Jesse, a kid who lived down the hall.

"You okay, man?" he asked when I opened the door.

"Yeah," I said. "I'm fine."

"I thought someone was in here," he said. "I heard you shouting the word 'go.'"

"Oh," I said. "Yeah, there was no one in here. I was just shouting the word 'go.'"

"Why?"

"No reason, okay?" I said, in a huff. "I just felt like shouting the word 'go.' Jesus, everyone is so fucking nosy here."

"Uhh . . . ," he squeaked out. "Sorry, man. Didn't mean to interrupt you . . . while you were shouting the word 'go.'"

I slammed the door and tumbled back into bed. I lifted my shaft once more.

"Please," I said, my rage turning into desperation. "Just a little bit. Just enough that she won't get grossed out." When I woke up I checked and, sure enough, no hair had grown. This process repeated itself every night. My penis refused to listen to reason. Or begging. Or shouting. My penis would not be swayed.

The day before I headed home to New Jersey, Samantha and I told each other how excited we were, and how we couldn't wait to see one another.

She was being honest. I was outright lying. Because due to my pubeless state I never wanted to go home, and I certainly never wanted to face her. The phone thing was great. I was able to say all sorts of heartfelt, risky stuff and there was no consequence. I was in total control. All I could think of was that once I saw her again in person I was going to be exposed as a sham, as a little boy, in the emotional and—more importantly—the physical sense. I could only imagine the shock, the disgust, the horror that she would feel if she reached into my pants and felt a man's front that felt like a baby's ass.

The drive back home was unbearable. With each hour on the highway bringing me closer to Jersey and the inevitable unveiling of my bald crotch, my panic grew. In my state of depression, I decided it would have been better if I had thrown up all over Samantha's face that day months ago. That way she never would have spoken to me again, and I wouldn't be in this whole mess of her wanting to provide me with hand release.

I finally got home, and within hours Samantha was at my front door. She looked great. I don't know if it was a result of her diligent bulimia, but she seemed more toned than usual. She was also tanned from a summer spent at the beach—three weeks of thus far shunning every guy who tried to convince her to rendezvous beneath the boardwalk, all so she could be with me, a pubeless boy wonder who yelled at his own genitals.

In my parents' basement, I put on a movie—the John Cusack classic *Say Anything*, because I am completely unoriginal. We sat on opposite ends of the couch, but as the night progressed Samantha inched closer. The next thing I knew, her hand touched mine. And before I realized it I had experienced my first kiss.

It got aggressive fast. It was the sort of passion only fifteen-year-olds can summon after they've been apart and talking dirty to each other for a month.

Then, as suddenly as Samantha had instigated it, I stopped our make-out session. I turned away from Samantha's eager mouth and fixed my gaze onto the misadventures of Lloyd Dobler. I was scared to be discovered for the freak I was.

Samantha took a pillow and laid it on my lap, resting her head there. For the rest of the night I watched the movie, and she watched me. She smiled at me enticingly. There was no way to explain that I was terrified to open a very hairless Pandora's box. Samantha looked at me with three weeks' worth of build-up in her eyes, but I couldn't find it in me to risk a humiliation that would lead to a lifetime of insecurity. So Samantha simply sat, her head resting on a pillow that was balanced on my raging boner. Looking back now, I can understand that the situation couldn't have been comfortable for her, physically or socially.

As soon as the credits rolled, I headed for the stairs. My dad offered to drive Samantha home. I went along for the ride. She and my dad talked more than she and I did.

The next night, Samantha asked me to come to her place. Her turf. I dreaded the thought that she would feel more free to be aggressive. With Samantha in control things were bound to go further, and I was sure my lack of hair would finally be exposed to the world.

When I got to her house, Samantha's best friend Veronica was there. I wasn't sure why at first, but her presence there was off-putting to me. Then a rare male instinct kicked in, and I recognized that for the first time in my life I was being cock-blocked.

I was torn. On the one hand, I was relieved that I wouldn't have to deal with the prospect of making out with Samantha again. Sure, my cock had been blocked, but I had been actively searching for a way to block my cock on my own. On the other hand, it still hurt and I still felt shame.

Samantha took me quietly into the next room.

"Look," she said. "I'm so sorry to do this."

I looked down at the ground. I was completely aware of what was coming, but I was confused and unsure how to react. Did I pretend I was sad about what was happening? *Was* I sad? Was it embarrassing getting dumped after one date, or was it the biggest stroke of luck I'd yet experienced in my decade and a half on earth?

I went with what I thought was the smartest option—stoically absorbing the blow while hinting that there was a deep well of pain just under the surface. That way, Samantha would think I was some sort of sensitive guy, yet tough enough to weather a breakup.

I looked back up at Samantha.

"Just say whatever you have to say," I said.

"I really like you," she said. "But just as a friend. Something didn't quite click last night. Something was off. It was just. . . . "

It was just my boner stabbing your temple through a pillow, I thought to myself. *We both know it. Now. Let. Me. Go. Home.*

"It's over," she said. "I'm sorry."

She hugged me. And as she did I inhaled deeply and took in a strong waft of that unmistakable birch beer smell Samantha had long been famous for.

I walked by Veronica on my way out. She smiled at me, gently, not condescending at all. Her greenish-blue eyes spoke to a kindness that was very genuine. I stopped.

"I'll see you when school starts back up?" I said.

"Yeah," Veronica answered. "I'll see you then."

Then I gave her a very goofy grin. She laughed.

She's cuter anyway, I thought to myself.

As the summer wound down I kept up one of my rituals from debate camp. Each night, I stayed up late and examined my genitals for signs of hair. On occasion, I still quietly talked to them. And eventually, those hairs appeared. Within months, I would be blessed with a bright-red fire crotch that became its own source of embarrassment.

Over time I realized that while my lack of pubes had been *a* problem, it had never really been *the* problem.

The real issue was my awkward, clunky behavior. It was my nervousness, my uncomfortable shifting and sweating. It was my remarkable inability to deal with the situation in a straightforward way.

I had completely betrayed the attitude that had enticed Samantha in the first place. I had played it cool when I almost threw up on Samantha's head. But I couldn't play it cool when faced with the prospect of her seeing my hairless pubic mound. If I had figured out how to summon that same level-headedness, and managed to convert the impending disaster into another victory, we might have had a relationship that went somewhere.

I may at least have gotten a tug job out of it.

As an adult I've learned that even if there are moments when I feel I am mere seconds from vomiting on my life, I can still pull it together to regain control, and that good things can still come from it. On my best days, this helps. When it doesn't I can feel my same old insecurities set in—my awkwardness, my over-thought reactions to things, my inability to act when any action at all will turn a situation from tense to fine. It is a pattern that has reoccurred often, and it is in these instances that I feel like a frightened fifteen-year-old again, scared to take his eyes off the television screen, managing only to awkwardly jam his un-welcomed boner firmly into the temple of life.

Scared Straight

"I'm sorry, class," Henry Knutsen said as he stood at the front of the room. "Things are getting a little too serious in here." I shifted in my seat, giddy with anticipation. "Would anyone like to see me do my impression of bacon?"

We cheered. None of us anticipated this much fucking around when we signed up for a class on Law. Knutsen pinned his arms against his sides and jumped around as if he was a slice of pork frying in a pan. "I'm burning!" he shouted. "I'm burning!"

We clapped. Then he went back to teaching us about the Supreme Court.

Henry Knutsen had taught in West Orange for over forty years. At the beginning of my senior year, he announced that he would finally be retiring. For those of us who had already registered for his classes, this was a godsend. As far as we were concerned, Knutsen had effectively announced that he no longer gave a fuck about our education, and we couldn't have been happier.

When he wasn't impersonating breakfast meats, Knutsen figured out other ways to waste time, his favorite being *The*

Shawshank Redemption. That movie's long, and high school classes are short. We spent a good week watching a movie all of us had seen on TBS at least half a dozen times already. After the scene where Andy Dufresne escapes, Knutsen rewound the movie and had us rewatch the jailbreak ten times in a row. He never told us why. He just sighed each time with a far-off look in his eye.

Looking back, I realize that Knutsen must have seen a lot of himself in that moment. Andy Dufresne escaped Shawshank by using a rock to smash a hole in a pipe. He then climbed through a river of human shit and was finally free. I'm pretty sure that Knutsen saw his experience teaching at West Orange High as his own private prison. His retirement was his escape, and his final year with us was his slow crawl through a shit pipe.

And for this we loved him. But we also got the feeling that the school officials weren't quite as pleased. Many of us believed that they had in fact decided to make an example out of him; rather than allow him the opportunity to coast through his final year, one final victory lap half-heartedly incorporating his standard class routines, they made it clear that there would be no escaping so easily. Before he tasted freedom he would have to endure one final indignity. He would have to serve as the chaperone for that year's trip to the Scared Straight program.

"Well, kids," he told us, "I won't be in class next Wednesday because I'm being forced to go to prison. Prison has a lot to do with law. Would anyone like to volunteer and come along?" I looked around. No one raised their hands.

Except me. I was shocked. Was no one else interested in seeing the inside of a jail? For about 80 percent of the people in the class, this was probably the only time they'd have that opportunity. I needed to go. Both for curiosity's sake and for the sake of getting the reaction I got upon raising my hand. Classmates nervously glanced in my direction. It brought joy to my soul seeing that volunteering for a trip to the bowels of incarceration freaked them out—it meant they were reevaluating me. That made me happy, even if they now thought I was a little bit crazy. Willfully entering the New Jersey penal system was one of the worst ideas I'd had in a while. That's why I liked it.

Later that week, I slipped a piece of paper to my mom while we ate dinner.

"Class trip," I said, trying to get the process done without her actually reading the permission slip. "Need you to sign this."

"Rahway State Prison?" she asked. "What the hell is this?"

"Scared Straight," I said. "I'm volunteering to go."

"Are you out of your mind?" my mother asked.

"Let him go," my father said. "Maybe it'll do him some good."

Before we go any further, I think you should know something. At the time, this is what I looked like, roughly:

I say "roughly" because I'd also exacerbated my obvious and numerous social problems by dyeing my hair bright red. So not only was I a seventeen-year-old who looked like an eleven-year-old, but my hair was a ludicrously vibrant scarlet. Which is good, because I think we'd all agree that I don't look feminine enough in that picture.

If this story were fictional, it would probably be titled "Encyclopedia Brown and a Bus Full of Thugs Visit a State Prison." Unfortunately, it was my real life.

We weren't going to just any prison. We were visiting Rahway State. This is the jail where the original Scared Straight film was produced. That film has since been condemned for encouraging wholly ineffective behavior that was deemed borderline child abuse. For a guy looking to see the genuinely fucked-up parts of life, it was perfect.

I sat at the front of the bus with Knutsen. He stared out the window, ignoring us, undoubtedly dreaming of finding his personal Red and moving to a beach where they could build wooden boats. I realized that we had a lot in common. Here was a mild-mannered guy just like me, glasses and all. He felt stuck and wanted to get out, just like I did. The only difference was that he had put up with this for decades. Knutsen was exactly the type of guy I was expected to turn into. His visible frustrations were the future I feared. The part of me that climbed onto that bus was the crazy side that would not accept such a fate.

The kids in the back shouted things such as "Yo Knutsen! Call ahead and tell them I'm coming! Warn those prisoners they need to be scared of me!" and the simpler but just as effective "I ain't scared of shit, so fuck this." But I knew better. While I would go home to a relatively normal life that afternoon, their problems ran deeper. After all, they didn't volunteer for the trip. From Kenward, a badass rumored to have thrown an Indian dwarf down a staircase, to Frank the loudmouthed football player who thought the rules didn't apply to him, this was the murderer's row of the West Orange High class of '98. But on the

bus, I sensed a different side of all of them. Their verbal sparring might have sounded tough, but there was a subtext of desperation and fear. They seemed sad and insecure outside the
context of a high school.

When we pulled up to Rahway State, the bluster and posturing stopped. The prison was huge, surrounded by guard towers
and fences and covered in barbed wire. Quiet fell over the bus as
we all asked the same unspoken question: *If it's this bad outside,
what must it be like inside?*

Fear punched me in the gut. I was in over my head. I considered asking Knutsen if I could stay on the bus, but before I could,
three surly prison guards leapt onboard.

"Everyone sit the fuck down and shut the fuck up!" they
screamed. It was clear that these men had no qualms about mur-
dering any of us. "I dare someone to talk! Give me a reason to
spill some brains on the ground, I'd fucking love that!"

A shocked silence spread among the crowd and we sat down.

"Now stand the fuck up!" We leapt from our seats. They had us
under control immediately; we sat when they told us, we stood
when they told us. As they herded us into a concrete pen and
made us stand in a single-file line, I understood that they were
treating us as badly as any prisoner. Though I tried to stay stoic
and calm, I shook like a Parkinson's patient who has recently been
given tragic news. Knutsen was nowhere to be found. The only
other noncriminal from my school was gone. I was on my own.

The guards ran up and down the line, screaming at us. I
winced, shocked that they were treating me exactly the same as
everyone else. I had figured that someone would call ahead and
tell them, *"Hey, go all out on these guys, except there's one volunteer, so take it easy on him. You'll know him when you see him—
he's the one who wears sweater vests and looks like he's really into*

Morrissey." No one had placed that call. I was bearing the brunt of things as much as anyone else.

When the kid in front of me noticed my trembling, he whispered, "Stay still, merigon." For years, I thought that "merigon" was a derogatory way to call someone an American, like "gringo." Only recently did I learn that it's the Spanish word for "faggot."

The guards walked the line, holding up Polaroids of inmates who'd committed suicide. Mostly they'd hanged themselves with bed sheets, but one particularly gruesome image showed a man who had sharpened a broomstick and impaled it through his own neck.

Well, I thought to myself, *I guess this is real life.*

My shaking grew. I breathed in heavy gasps, sweating as the guards brought us into the general-population area. A group of prisoners folded laundry inside a cage. When they saw us they dropped the clothes and sheets and ran to the bars, screaming.

I first realized they were shouting at me personally when one guy remained conspicuously silent and made eye contact with me. As our eyes locked he shouted just loudly enough for me to hear it: "I'm gonna fuck you, Red. I'm gonna fuck you."

I almost shit my pants with fear. My hope was that the eventual loss of my virginity would be a tender and loving affair. If this man had his way it would be violent, bloody, and nonconsensual. I'd never felt so unprotected. And seeing the rage in the eyes of this unapologetic rapist dwarfed any anger I'd ever known. We'd been on the prison grounds less than five minutes and I'd already learned what I wanted to know: I wasn't tough, no one in my school was tough, no one I would ever meet again for the rest of my life would be tough in comparison to these men. I wanted to go home.

We went on a whirlwind tour of the prison, every step scarier than the last. The guards locked us inside a small cell with a prisoner. We stood crammed against each other in one corner as the man laughed and stared us down.

"Anybody want to try any fucking funny shit?" he asked. No one budged. "Didn't think so," he grinned.

We were shuffled into a dark auditorium and told to sit on our knees with our hands under our butts. The cavernous room was black save for the light on the stage.

"Stay right where you are, and don't put your hands anywhere but under your assholes," the guards said. "We're leaving. But don't worry—the lifers are on their way."

The lifers were the group of murderers at the heart of Scared Straight. Before we'd left on this trip, Knutsen had made it very clear that these were very dangerous men.

"Keep in mind the lifers will yell at you," he'd said on the bus, "but they can't touch you. If they do, the guards will take them out. Hard. Because it will be bad."

My mouth went dry.

"The reason they can't touch you is because they once put a kid in the hospital," he continued. "Not someone from our school. Thank God. It sounds like the sort of thing you wouldn't want to see with your own eyes."

There wasn't a single faker amongst the lifers; these were authentic killers—murderers who had killed and gone to prison, and who would one day die in prison.

The door burst open. A dozen of the hardest-looking men I've ever seen walked in and glared at us. They made eye contact, intimidating us even before speaking.

I glanced out of the corner of my eye at my classmates. Looking down the line, I saw bully after bully, each more formidable than the last. At the end of the line was Kenward. I'd never seen him look anything but aggressive. He was as scared as I was.

Finally, one of the inmates stepped forward and talked.

He seemed reasonable enough. I mean, he was still scary as shit, but within the bounds of reason. "You kids think you're bad, I guess," he began. "Well, let me tell you something. Crime is a road I've walked down. And it's a dark road."

With no provocation he turned into a cross between the Incredible Hulk and the Ultimate Warrior. "AND YOU DON'T WANT TO *WALK* DOWN THAT *ROAD!*" He shouted in a low guttural roar. His eyes bulged out of his head like Beetlejuice, and when he reared back and flexed his muscles, veins popped out of his arms and neck. He was easily the scariest person I'd ever seen. If it wasn't so clearly legit, his scariness would have been cartoonish. I was tempted to laugh, but was smart enough not to tempt this man's ire.

Frank the loudmouthed jock didn't demonstrate the same restraint. He smirked. After all the day's events, I didn't know why he thought this was a good idea. Frank wasn't the worst guy, just kind of a punk. He was a good-looking mixed-race athlete who saw himself as the shit and got in trouble trying to prove it. As soon as he smirked, the inmate was in his face. "Why you laughing, motherfucker? You think we boys?" he asked. "Why, 'cause you black? You ain't black, you half a nigga!"

Frank burst into tears. Seeing this football player break down so easily—a guy who could probably bench-press me— made a lightbulb go off in my brain: toughness is a defense mechanism, and all of us are just trying to make it through the day. It was the first time I'd ever felt a bond with Frank: we both had the ability to cry like little bitches.

A kid none of us recognized was led in to join us halfway through the endless parade of screaming murderers. His parents had brought him. He didn't go to our school and was four or five years younger than us. He had a bad look about him.

Apparently the prisoners had been told to go hard on this kid. They got in his face, threatened him physically, and actually pushed him around. As he sobbed, a few of them lifted him up and another prisoner tore his sneakers from his feet. He flung the shoes into the auditorium's seats. We watched the sneakers disappear into total darkness and listened to them land with a clatter among the chairs.

Well this is it, I thought to myself. *You're finally gonna see someone get killed.*

They put the kid back down on the ground and he collapsed, a crying mess.

Then the scariest prisoners made their way to the back of the stage and sat down. A shy-looking skinny kid stepped forward. His voice was soft and gentle. "I'm nineteen years old," he began. "I'm only a few years older than you guys." After an afternoon of shock-and-awe-style intimidation, this emotional attack was the knockout punch.

"I want you to think about what you're doing," he said. "I wish I could be where you're at. You guys are gonna go to college next year. I'll never get to. You're gonna go to parties, with girls. I'll never go to a college party."

A sick, twisting pain burned in my gut as I met eyes with the kid. His baby face was evident despite the prison uniform and heavy boots. He looked like a kid dressed up as one of the other prisoners for Halloween.

"So stop fucking up," he said. "Because I would take back everything I did to be where you guys are at right now." And then he cried. We sat for the longest minute of our lives, staring at the ground. Throughout the entire afternoon, we'd been barraged with threats and screaming. It was only during this sickening silence that we had the opportunity to finally start thinking again.

This, I thought to myself, *is fucking depressing.*

My schoolmates were shell-shocked. Frank was so pale that he looked 100 percent Caucasian. Kenward's lumbering frame was slumped over in defeat. With the tension having hit its peak, we began to shift on our heels. We were ready to leave.

"You motherfuckers stay right the fuck where you are," one of the prisoners snapped. "Crazy Chris ain't got here yet. He'll be here any second now."

Once again the room fell silent, and this time the prisoners themselves looked uncomfortable. Whoever Crazy Chris was, he bothered even the other murderers.

The door bounced open with a well-placed kick. In walked Crazy Chris, a white man in his early sixties. A grizzled beard was the only masculine thing about him, as his other accoutrements included lipstick and women's clothes. *That*, I told myself, *is a very bad man.* Once again my classmates and I shared uncertain glances, all of us wondering the same thing: *Who survives in a place like this dressed like that?* Earlier, I felt like I was going to get murdered for having red hair. This dude wore *lipstick* and everyone else was scared of *him.* To even get your hands on women's clothes in a men's prison you had to be a shady motherfucker. To survive in them, you had to be a badass. To not only survive but to incite fear in other inmates, you must be the craziest of the crazy. This guy may very well have been the baddest man in New Jersey.

He took center stage and grinned a toothless grin at us.

"My name is Crazy Chris." He paused for dramatic effect. "And sometimes, my dick gets hard like Christmas candy." No one moved, no one swayed, no one even breathed. I shut my eyes and prayed that when I opened them he would be gone. He wasn't. Instead, he kneeled inches away from the face of a classmate. "What happens to Christmas candy?" he asked the boy. The kid didn't answer. Fire grew in Crazy Chris's eyes. "I SAID, WHAT HAPPENS TO CHRISTMAS CANDY?"

The kid realized he wasn't getting off the hook.

"It . . ."—he shut his eyes with the realization of what level of shame he was about to reach—"it gets sucked." His voice broke as he said it.

"That's right," Crazy Chris said. "Christmas candy gets sucked." And with that, he walked out the door. No lesson, no moral, nothing like the other guys had given us. Just a threat of mouth rape and he was out. The guards came back and shuffled us away, and soon the gates shut behind us as we trembled in shock.

Thirty seconds after we got back on the bus, the thugs got back to business.

"Knutsen," someone shouted, "call them bitches back and tell them I said fuck you." Knutsen smirked. He knew he was days away from his escape. I smiled, knowing that I would never feel the satisfaction he was feeling, because I would never put myself in a position to need it. Knutsen and I were similar people in many ways. We were both nerdy, stiff, socially awkward goofballs. It was easy to imagine his present as my future. Seeing the frustration all over his face, watching him come into class every day resigned and defeated, I knew I had to avoid that future at all costs. Knutsen was a very good man, but there was no way I could allow myself to fall into a similarly dreary routine.

In that sense, Scared Straight worked on me. I've also never been incarcerated, though admittedly I wasn't a high-risk candidate.

It's for the best. I don't even like Christmas candy.

Virginity

I spent the first seventeen years of my life firmly believing that my penis would never know the smooth, moist contours of vaginal walls.

This wasn't an outlandish thought. I grew up in North Jersey. The people who became sexually active at a young age were tanned and athletic and chewed their gum loudly. I was pale and shy and never managed to run with the sort of crowd that spent their middle school years fucking in public parks.

My father never gave me "the talk." To this day, I don't think he's ever acknowledged the existence of sex in my presence. He's more concerned with things like Steven Seagal movies and the pH balance of the water in our backyard pool. One time around 1999, he mumbled something about "hope you're careful." That's the only indication I've ever received that he recognizes sexual activity is a real thing I might actually partake in.

My mother once tried to broach the subject, but it was a vague, off-putting discussion. I was on the phone in our kitchen, and when I hung up she was sitting at the table waiting to speak with me.

"You know, your body's going to start changing soon," she said.

"Yeah, I know," I replied.

She paused. She looked down, her eyes scanning the table for some hint of what to do or say. She looked back up.

"Sometimes I find stuff in your brother's sheets," she blurted out.

She grimaced. I grimaced. We looked away from each other.

"What do you do?" I finally asked.

"I throw them in the laundry machine!" she said, before standing and literally running away.

My aforementioned brother, two years my senior, could have served as my guide to matters such as these, but frankly, he wasn't much help. Most brothers probably had heart-to-hearts about sex and girls and whatnot. My brother and I had bigger fish to fry.

After he left for LaSalle University, a typical phone conversation with him would go like this: "Yo," he'd start out, "can you believe Jerry the King Lawler showed up in ECW? He's a WWF guy!"

"You meet any girls down there?" I would try to slip in.

"Nah," he would quickly say. "But can you believe that Cactus Jack took that bump from Sabu? Man, ECW is the best."

Even if Gregg was more concerned with filling me in on the events of the third most popular professional wrestling league in America than with talking about girls, he still could have given me slivers of advice along the way. Where was I supposed to take girls on dates, for example? Where should I go to meet them in the first place? (I still have no idea.) And what about what to wear? Not that his suggestions would necessarily have helped.

The most fashion conscious my brother ever got was when our neighbor gave him a huge bag of clothes from the early '70s that had been stored away in his garage.

"Holy shit," Gregg said as he rifled through it and took out one particularly hideous item. "This orange jumpsuit is made of corduroy. Perfect!"

He wore that orange corduroy jumpsuit all through his senior year of high school, which was the same year I was a freshman. While dressing like a member of Devo might have spoken to Gregg's free spirit, the female reactions to it that I saw firsthand made it absolutely clear he would not and should not be my mentor in the ways of love.

By the time my own senior year of high school rolled around, when my brother's performance-art style of dress had mercifully faded to just a distant memory, I had established a pattern of how I dealt with women. It was a simple three-step process.

1. Fall in love with a girl and absolutely never ever tell her.
2. Slowly become her "best friend" over the course of a few months.
3. Wait until she told me a guy had asked her out and she said yes. (At which point I would break down and tell her I loved her. To which she would reply she thought we were just good friends. To which I would explain that I'd always felt this way, and here she would accurately point out that I had been deceptive and manipulative by not revealing my true intentions. Afterward, we wouldn't talk much anymore. Then back to step 1 and repeat.)

It fit me like a glove. I was good at that routine. From Kristy Enginger to Melissa Goldfarb and back again, I was an old pro.

Then I met Veronica and she fucked it all up by actually liking me back.

Veronica was a redheaded, freckle-faced Irish Catholic girl. She was amazingly kind and cute. She'd also spent her whole childhood doing Irish step dancing, so her body was tighter than any seventeen-year-old's has a right to be.

The first actual conversation I'd had with Veronica was the one that occurred as I sadly left her best friend Samantha's house after Samantha dumped me for delivering one of the most awkward first kisses in human history.

During our junior year of high school, Veronica and I hit it off. She found me funny. I found her leggy and redheaded. I put my usual plan into action. It didn't take too many months before we were talking on the phone every night. I liked her so much that when I heard things like the following—

"I don't care if I play cymbals and Kevin Connolly plays quads. I work harder than him and I should be the sole drum captain. It's bullshit. We're the only section in the whole marching band with two captains."

—I was able to pretend I actually gave a fuck. *That's* love.

Toward the end of the year I found myself on the phone with a guy named Will. He was an all right guy, but he was a little stiff and didn't have much of a sense of humor. He also played the trumpet and was Unitarian. To this day I literally know nothing about the Unitarian religion, but I can safely say that the phrase "Unitarian trumpeter" doesn't sound like the sort of label you'd attach to someone who's fun to date.

"Hey, you're friends with Veronica," he said.

"Yeah, good friends. Best friends," I answered.

"I asked her out the other day and she said yes. Any tips on what she likes?"

Up until then, I had kept my crush on Veronica secret from everyone. But Will must have instantly realized it existed. It wasn't hard to deduce, being that my response was a long pause followed by muffled sobs.

"Are you crying?" he asked, clearly annoyed.

"Yes," I replied, figuring there was no reason to lie about it at this point.

"You like her, don't you?" He sighed, heavily. "Let's solve this right now."

Then, before I knew exactly what was happening, Will dialed Veronica up on three-way. She picked up to hear her boyfriend of nine hours and her weepy best friend on the line together. With him listening, I poured my heart out to her.

"It's just," I sobbed, "I think you're so nice, and you're beautiful, and we have so much fun together, and I've wanted to ask you out for so long, but I never was brave enough, and I wish I was, because now I maybe lost my chance and I just can't handle—"

Wisely, she cut me off.

"Chris," she said. "I don't think it would work anyway. You're my best friend, and I need you for that. But we wouldn't work together."

"So we cool?" Will said. I wanted to reach through the phone and strangle him.

Somehow, though, life went on.

Veronica and Will dated for nine brutally long months. As summer moved forward and we entered our senior year, I couldn't shake my crush on Veronica.

Strangely, and independently of all of this, I somehow became just a tiny bit popular during my final year of high school.

The head of the cheerleading team, Debbie, was my lab partner in physics class, based purely on the fact that the only other available option left was a Greek guy known as "Shit Lip Larry." Debbie and I sat together, and at first she cold-shouldered me. But the teacher of the class was a club-foot-stricken creep named David Harding whom everyone called Mr. Hard-on. He had a habit of bothering female students. Debbie was at the top of his list.

"If you apply that formula, you'll see how fast the plane rises despite gravity," he'd say, grinning at Debbie as he leaned over our table and pointed toward a physics worksheet. "Sometimes things rise real fast. . . . Real fast. . . . "

"Mr. Hard-on, I got a question," I jumped in and said.

"Fine," he grumbled, turning his attention to me.

"How much force does it take for a roller coaster to go in a loop, and also do you think the way you're behaving is appropriate?"

I was trying to be a wiseass mostly to break the tension, but as a side effect Debbie came to find me both funny and a pretty good guy.

When people noticed that she and I were palling around, it gave me credibility among a whole new social class. For the first time, those tanned, athletic gum chewers had decided I was okay enough to hang around their periphery. It gave me a bit more confidence.

At year's end, Veronica and Will were still dating. But she somehow broke rule 3 of my well-trod cycle. Instead of feeling betrayed or duped by my feelings toward her, Veronica actually made an effort to remain friends.

We even still hung out. Albeit in a platonic way.

She worked a few nights a week as the receptionist at the rectory of a church. She was convinced that a ghost haunted the building. While terrifying for Veronica, this was great for me. She'd sit on the phone with me all night to avoid getting too scared.

I did my part to be a good guy and make her feel better, but don't think for one fucking second that I wasn't fanning those flames every chance I got.

"You know," I said. "Ghosts respond the most to teenaged girls."

"Shut up," Veronica answered. "You're just saying that to scare me."

"Well, I *am* trying to scare you," I admitted. "But I saw a show about it on the History Channel. For real. Girls between fourteen and seventeen drive ghosts completely nuts."

After enough of these conversations, she hit her breaking point. One late evening I was off on some tangent about how ghosts are sometimes good and sometimes bad, but poltergeists are always bad, when she interrupted me.

"Could you come up here to keep me company?" she asked.

"Yeah," I answered, barely concealing my glee. "No problem."

I drove from my house up to Livingston, where we sat in the church basement together. I made fun of her about the haunting and tried to scare her. Before I knew it, we were holding each other on the couch because she was "scared of the ghost."

This happened a few weeks in a row. Eventually, we were cuddling without even the pretext of fearing the supernatural.

One night she was lying on my lap.

"I'm not saying Kevin Connolly is a bad guy," she said. "I'm just saying that he doesn't need to be drum captain. If he wanted to be, he should have—"

"You know," I interrupted. "Sometimes it's really hard for me to stop myself from kissing you."

Veronica looked back at me.

"Then why don't you just do it?"

And I did.

"God," she said. "I can't believe I'm making out with you. This is so weird."

"What do you mean?" I asked.

"I just never thought you'd be interested in me," she replied.

This baffled me to no end, as she was one of the three participants in a conference call that had led to roughly nine months of horrifically low self-esteem for me.

"Are you kidding me?" I replied. "I've been chasing you for a year."

"That was a year ago," she said. "You're, like, cool now."

She broke things off with Will and we became an item. Veronica was my first everything. We dated for years, and I learned much about life during my time with her. We had ups and downs like anyone else, and I'm willing to admit that 99 percent of what went wrong in that relationship was my fault. But the one thing I will always blame her for is the way in which we lost our virginity to each other.

Fact: Any nerd you meet spends his childhood being completely sex obsessed. It doesn't matter whether he's a comic book nerd or a Dungeons & Dragons nerd or a fantasy baseball nerd or some terribly pitiful combination of all the different kinds of nerd-dom. A nerd is a nerd and he will have thought about sex for hours each day starting at the age of thirteen. Why? Because there's no visible light at the end of the tunnel assuring a nerd that one day he actually will have sex.

Like all humans, nerds want what they can't have. And they are obsessive people by nature. So my recommendation to any ladies, if you wind up dating a nerd virgin as Veronica once did, is to let the first time sweep over both of you spontaneously. Allow it to be of the moment, to be a surprise.

Certainly don't pull your boyfriend aside and whisper, "I've decided I want to lose my virginity to you. *Let's do it in a week.*"

Because then you will have just made sure that nerd is going to have the worst week of his life.

You will have sentenced him to spend the next seven days— the next 168 hours—obsessing over the idea that it's *finally going to happen.*

As a result, he is also going to spend those seven days reading up on cunnilingus and sex positions and ejaculation etiquette. About how he's going to . . . maybe get a girl pregnant. He is going to research every STD over and over again, because he's a nerd, and that means he loves gathering information and minutia, even if it's about the many different types of warts that can grow on the underside of a penis head.

That is how I spent my last week as a virgin. Nervous, skittish, obsessed. Wondering and worrying about how it was going to go.

In the middle of that week, I decided it was time to face the reality of the situation and that I needed to get prepared.

I needed to buy condoms.

I borrowed my mom's car and drove around town. Every time I got to a pharmacy, I pulled into the parking lot and convinced myself that I absolutely could not buy condoms there. Some of my justifications were very rational.

This is Veronica's neighborhood, I thought to myself. *What if her dad sees me buying condoms?*

The first time I met Veronica's father, he explained to me that he had served in World War II. He then went on to tell me he worked at a VCR company.

"I find it funny," he said, combining the two thoughts. "I used to kill those people. Now I work for them."

When your girlfriend's father has taken human life, I contend it's okay to avoid purchasing condoms in his neighborhood. Unfortunately, some of my other reasons for dodging the transaction weren't so logical.

Mom went to high school with the ex-husband of a lady who lives on the other side of that mountain there, I remember thinking while sitting in my car behind the CVS drugstore on Eagle Rock Avenue. *If she sees me, reunites with her ex-husband after seven years of divorce, and he randomly contacts my mother for the first time in twenty-eight years, I'm so dead!*

My only option, as I saw it, was to buy my condoms far from where any family, friends, or associates could find me. I knew of a Pathmark located in the basement of an old converted train station in a nearby town. I figured that Pathmark would have a pharmacy and that the odds were good no one I had ever met in my entire life would have a reason to be hanging out inside a faraway subterranean Pathmark.

I got out of my car and headed to the entrance, only to turn around and walk right back to my car. I sat down in the driver's seat.

"No," I said to myself, out loud. "You have got to do this."

Despite my best efforts to mentally overcome my embarrassment, my body did not respond to my words. I remained sitting.

"If you can't do this," I said, "then you can't do *it*."

Begrudgingly, my body finally cooperated and I walked back toward the front entrance. This time I made it inside, and headed straight to the pharmacy.

Then, I panicked. I walked around the border of the pharmacy, orbiting the condoms, for ten full minutes. I didn't look at any other items, and only managed to examine the condoms by turning my head and reading the packages as I speed-walked past them. Otherwise, I kept my head down and continued my loop around the edge of the pharmacy.

The workers behind the counter, two heavyset black women, were eyeing me, confused. They must have thought that I was out of my mind, or that I found supermarket pharmacies a great place to run laps.

After I tired out, and not coincidentally after every other customer had left the pharmacy, I buckled down and made my way back toward the condoms. The choice was overwhelming, but I'd done my research and came knowing what I wanted: regular condoms with one simple frill, spermicidal lubricant. Without thinking about what I was doing, I saw my hand reach for them. I picked them up, nervously walked to the checkout, and looked at the ground as the woman behind the counter rang up my purchase.

She continued making small talk with her coworker. Neither seemed to even notice me, and I liked that. I was doing my best to avoid eye contact and remain as nondescript as possible. I just wanted to get done with my purchase and be on my way. Remarkably, at first it seemed as simple as any other transaction I'd partaken in before that extremely terrifying one. I pushed my money across the counter, and she pushed back my change, along with a crinkly white paper bag that held a box containing my first three prophylactics. Simple as that. In and out.

But I was wrong. The woman behind the counter did in fact take notice of me.

As I walked out of the pharmacy, when she assumed I was out of earshot (she clearly hadn't taken into account my adrenaline-fueled hyper-senses), she made a simple statement that tore me to pieces.

"He ain't ready."

She declared it to her friend, off-handedly. "He ain't ready."

I heard it, and I bolted.

Outside I sat in my car and cried because I knew she was right.

In the remaining days before the big night, I did my best to damn well *get* ready. In my little blue box, I had three condoms. I would need one for the act. I'd need a second one in case the first one broke.

This left me with one condom to practice with.

Late that night, when my parents had gone to sleep, I sat on the couch in our basement trembling with fear. I removed one of the condoms from the box. I opened it, looked at it, and unrolled it. It wasn't as difficult to put on as I thought it would be.

Now, to practice something like this isn't that weird. In fact, it's sort of responsible. But it's hard to decide if what I did next was more gross or bizarre.

I took the condom off and held it in my palm. In my panic-fueled obsession, I'd decided that I needed to practice putting it on as many times as possible. So instead of tossing it I rolled it back onto my dick and pulled it back off three or four times.

Then I decided I should practice more tomorrow.

I went into our basement bathroom, which no one really used, and wrapped it in toilet paper. I opened the cabinet under the sink and placed it in the far back corner.

For the next three nights, I retrieved that condom and placed it back on my dick close to three dozen times.

I have since realized how bizarre these practice runs were, but when you're as stressed as I was, you'll do funny things. Or unsanitary, gross things, as was the case with that rehearsal rubber. Gross or not, though, it did the trick. By the time Saturday night came, I was mentally prepared to get a condom on when it counted.

Veronica came over to my house late that night. She looked beautiful. We went swimming in the aboveground pool next to the garage in my backyard.

"Are you sure you want to do this?" I asked her as we floated quietly on the surface of the water.

"Of course I do," she answered. She took my hand in hers. "It's you."

When she said that, for the first time in a week I stopped feeling nervous. She was right. I pulled her toward me and we made out.

There, in what was basically a big backyard bucket, where any of my neighbors could have looked out of their windows and seen, I received a delicate half of a handjob and I dispensed my very fumbly, awkward fingers to her genital regions as well. Veronica was aggressive, and I was going with it. I could tell that she'd spent the week mulling over this decision as well. And we'd both come to the same conclusion: tonight was the night our mutual virginity would be lost. We were nervous, we were turned on, and we were going for it.

We got out of the pool. I dried her off and then toweled myself down. We climbed up the wooden steps of my back porch, and I held open the aluminum door for her. Inside, we quickly went downstairs to the basement.

There, on a gray checker-patterned couch, set against the fake-pine paneling of the wall and enveloped in the glow of my basement's aquarium, we lost our virginity to each other in perhaps the most suburban way possible.

Practice paid off. The condom went on without incident.

When we were done we lay next to one another for a while. I thought about speaking, but there was nothing to say. We remained still, our two naked bodies crammed awkwardly next to each other on the thin couch. I listened to Veronica breathing. I tried to take a moment to think about what had just happened, but I couldn't. In a good way. For possibly the first time in my life, my mind was totally clear.

Eventually, I got up and went to the bathroom in the corner of the basement. When I headed back to the couch I knelt down next to Veronica.

"Are you okay?" she asked me.

"Yeah," I said. "Are you?"

She nodded at me and smiled. Then, with my trademark wisdom and great timing, I blurted out, "You're bleeding."

"Oh," she said, her smile fading.

"Did you know that?" I asked. "You're bleeding. I can tell, because when I took off the condom, there was blood, and—"

"Chris," she interrupted me, sternly. "Stop talking. I'll take care of it." She shook her head and then laughed. It was the first time I realized that in order to date me, you have to find social awkwardness funny. To this day, I have never had a relationship work if that rule wasn't quickly realized and understood.

When she got up and went to the bathroom to check on herself, I sat down on the couch. I was still holding the used condom in my hand. I picked up the wrapper it came in. I balled up the condom and its foil sheath, and walked over to the garbage can. I shoved all of the evidence of my entrance into manhood into the hole of a discarded can of Diet Dr. Pepper.

There, I knew, my mother would never find it.

A Bad Idea I'm About to Do

Just after I left for my first year of college, my parents sold our house and I was faced with the reality that I could never go home again. Weeks after I arrived on campus, three deaths—one of a high school classmate, one of a family friend, one of a childhood playmate—followed in quick succession. On top of this, I was slowly discovering I was next in line to continue the family tradition of being bipolar, and was not dealing with it well.

Nothing delivered a bigger blow to my mental and emotional state, however, than my incredibly foolish decision to attend Rutgers University. As the premier state university of New Jersey, Rutgers has a proud history. It is one of nine colleges that existed in the United States during the colonial era. Among its alumni are Paul Robeson, Milton Friedman, and the dude who discovered antibiotics. But walking around campus after my arrival there, I soon came to realize that 1998 was a low point for the school. The crumbling buildings were a sign that the school wasn't the academic stalwart it once was, and the mind-boggling amount of construction sites pointed toward a rebuilt future that I would unfortunately not be around to enjoy.

Rutgers during my stay was both overcrowded and filthy. My dorm was perched up against the Raritan River, so that light-brown malaria pit was the view from my room. My roommate was an Estonian nationalist known as "the Russian Bear." The very best thing Rutgers had going for it, as far as I was concerned, was a group of trailers called "the Grease Trucks." They sold sandwiches, including one called a "Fat Bitch" that contained a cheesesteak, fries, mozzarella sticks, and chicken fingers. Let me reiterate—this was *the best thing the place had going for it*. Not that I had a right to be choosy. My main reason for going to Rutgers was that they didn't make me write an essay as part of the application.

Looking back on it now, I realize Rutgers and I had a lot in common: in a few years we would turn out fine, but back then we were both feeling pretty beat up. In the midst of that first semester, however, it was hard for me to see the bright side. In truth, I was miserable.

I tried to explain to my mom how unhappy I was.

"You've only been there five weeks," she replied, her voice devoid of sympathy.

"I mean, Mom," I said, "last night, a fat Asian guy threw up spaghetti in the showers and then tried to make out with me."

I registered the pause as my mother attempted to process the fact that homosexuals not only existed but also talked to her son. "I don't think you should tell me that, Chris," she said quietly.

My father, Johnny Education, was no help either. He went to Montclair State, near our house, and he would often tell stories about his time there.

"I worked every day stocking shelves," he'd say. "Then, at the end of my shift, I'd drive over there and take night classes. I was tired all the time."

He graduated in three years. Then he went on to get two master's degrees and an MBA. He recently received his PhD. Needless to say, my complaints about wanting to leave school were not the sort of thing I could talk to my dad about.

The next person I turned to was my usually reliable brother Gregg. After I told him how I was feeling, he drove to Rutgers and hung out in my dorm.

"So dude, what's going?" he asked upon arriving.

"Man, I don't know. I don't think this place is for me . . . at all," I answered.

"Cool," he said. "So how many girls live on your floor?"

Gregg's priorities were clearly not with helping his little brother.

With all of these factors lined up and pushing me into a very depressed corner, I did what anyone who was eighteen in the late '90s would do—I retreated to the Internet. Specifically, to AOL's Instant Messenger program.

At any moment I wasn't in class (my favorite that semester was "Dinosaurs," because every time it met, the professor would grab at his hair in frustration and shout, "They're just birds," over and over again) or at the dining hall (where my favorite meal—one that I ate at least once and sometimes twice a day—was four separate bowls of Cocoa Krispies, a plate of cheese fries, and copious amounts of cranberry juice), I was online, talking to friends from high school and my family. I was doing anything and everything to avoid dealing with the reality of my actual existence, so naturally I spent hours sitting at my computer.

My name online was "Framsky." And "Framsky," probably due to the fact that it's much easier to hide emotions in typed messages on a screen as opposed to actual conversations with real people, wasn't half as sad or miserable as "Chris" was. "Framsky" was getting me through many days, and even more nights. While other kids were going to dorm-sponsored get-to-know-you events, I could sit online and tell my high school friends how lame things like that were, and not have to admit that it was my own social anxiety keeping me from participating. When people invited me to parties, I could act busy in front of the computer screen instead of owning up to the fact I felt too uncomfortable in my own skin to do anything around that many people.

I would even IM with the kid who lived directly across the hall from me, a ridiculously tall half-Asian kid named Andy. I'm still not sure why Andy and I didn't just walk across the hall and hang out. A typical conversation looked like this:

FRAMSKY: how's it going?
ANDY: I have no friends here
FRAMSKY: me either
ANDY: brb, i am gonna go stare at the Indian girl with the rotten tomato tits

Such were the types of high-minded, empowering conversations that served as life rafts, keeping one's psyche afloat.

That is, until the day "Framsky" was taken away from me.

One December night at about eight, I got a message from an acquaintance of mine named Rob. Rob went to Princeton, but was a friend of some friends I had met at Rutgers.

"Chris!" his message read. "WATCH OUT!"

Before I could even finish typing and sending the word "why," over thirty strangers randomly messaged me with no provocation. While I was trying to sort out what Rob's message was about, and what the strange feeding frenzy of online messages was for, they all began to "warn" me. As any avid IM user knows, too many warnings means you get booted from the program. I was cut off.

Sitting there on a Friday night, lonely and depressed, a Fat Bitch working its way through my intestinal tracts, I found myself unable to access my precious Instant Messenger. Suddenly, a rage known only to those with Irish blood raised by a melodramatic mother in a neighborhood full of self-hating Catholics burst within me. Even though no one else was there—not even the Russian Bear—I looked up at my filthy, cracked ceiling and let out a scream.

I immediately ran to the phone and called the friends who had introduced me to Rob—or, as I knew him online, Prfsr-Frink. They gave me his number.

"Chris?" he answered. He knew I would be calling.

"Rob," I said, "what was that? I mean—what WAS that?"

"I'm sorry," he said. "This kid who lives on my floor, he's been doing that all day to people. He calls them IM bombs. He thinks it's really funny."

"IM bomb? Why? What did I do to him?" I asked.

"Nothing. He just organizes a bunch of people and they do it randomly," Rob said. "He came into my room and took your name. I didn't realize. I'm really sorry."

"Rob, what's the kid's deal?" I asked, my mood shifting from confusion to anger.

"Well, it's Deh-reek," he said. "You gotta understand, he's a good guy, but—"

"Why do you say his name like that?" I asked.

"Huh?"

"Deh-reek," I repeated. "I've never heard that name before."

"Well, it's spelled like Derek, but he pronounces it Dehr-eek," Rob answered.

The grievances were piling up quickly. Not only did he IM bomb me, this guy also pronounced his name pretentiously. But what truly sealed Derek's fate was the fact that he attended Princeton. Even the most self-loathing Rutgers students have a natural hatred for our Ivy League neighbors. We're blue-collared. They're blue-blooded. We don't like it.

"What's his deal again?" I asked.

"Well," Rob said, "he's from Toronto, and—"

I exploded into the phone. "This fucking Canadian fuck."

I don't have a problem with Canadians per se; in fact, I wish we had their health care system. But I do have a problem with any Canadian who thinks he's going to walk onto my turf, New Jersey, and pull a fast one on me. New Jersey may not be the prettiest place in the world, but it's mine.

"Rob, what's the name of your dorm?" I asked. He told me.

Then, I took action. I threw open my door and saw Andy sitting with his door open across the hall. Andy was as depressed and crazy as I was, plus he had a car.

"Andy," I said. He turned around. "Want to drive to Princeton and beat up some Princeton kid?"

He answered "Yes" instantaneously, and with surprisingly little emotion in his voice. He didn't even look surprised at my query. It was as if he had been waiting all night for someone to walk by and offer a midnight beating of a Princeton student.

We called our other friend Jeff, who came running over. The three of us dressed in black from head to toe—black puffy jackets, black pants, black wool hats. We got in Andy's car, and we were off—three true-blue Jersey kids on our way to Princeton.

"How far is it again?" Jeff asked, shifting uncomfortably in the back seat.

"Maybe thirty miles," Andy answered. Thirty miles was all that separated our shitball college from one of the most prestigious schools on earth.

~~~

"Whoa," I gasped when we finally pulled up alongside Princeton's gates.

"Yeah," Andy said. "It's fucking beautiful."

All three of us shook our heads. Princeton was the complete opposite of Rutgers.

"It's so clean," Jeff said. We were shocked that a school could be so grime-free.

Princeton was clearly not the type of place where you got in without writing an essay.

"We probably shouldn't have dressed in all black," Andy said.

It suddenly dawned on us that at Princeton, someone was likely to stand out if he wasn't wearing khaki pants. Rocking wannabe paramilitary gear wasn't the best choice if we wanted to go unnoticed. It was the type of place where people were probably mortified at the sight of jeans, let alone people dressed up like James Bond movie henchmen. We knew we had to act fast or the police would be on their way, but were chagrined to realize that Derek's dorm was located at the opposite side of campus from where we parked. We sprinted, knowing we probably wouldn't make it there without being swept up like the state-school trash we were.

Luckily for us, it was as if the Princetonites couldn't even see us. No one blinked. It's my assumption that we had the same effect on them as Columbus's ships did on the Indians—none. They couldn't even fathom that we existed in their reality.

We made our way to the dorm and found we needed a magnetic swipe card to enter. This surprised us—at Rutgers, anyone could just walk into any dorm at any time. We responded in the only way we could think of—we tried to kick the door down. It wouldn't give. A young gentleman in a pair of khakis and loafers saw us in our frustration and walked up to us.

"Need to get inside?" he asked, smiling. He looked like an average turn-of-the-twenty-first-century preppy type, but his tone of voice was like Potsy or Dennis the Menace, something from a more innocent time. Clearly, this Princeton student had never tasted a Fat Bitch. He'd yet to have his optimistic outlook crushed by the harsh realities of life, like ours had.

"Yeah," we each grunted in a low guttural tone, the kind produced by months of damaging our throats with malt liquor, and hinting at the insomnia caused by the despair of our general direction.

He swiped us right in, apparently not sensing that we were clearly up to no good.

When we had left for Princeton, we planned on scaring Derek good. We didn't really think we were going to do any serious damage to him. But what we saw in the lobby of that immaculate, pristinely maintained dorm changed a lot of things for us that night, and sadly, a lot of things for Derek.

Gathered in the middle of the dorm were a group of about fifteen kids. Every single one of them was wearing a sweater and/or turtleneck. They were standing around the dorm's *grand piano. Grand. Piano.*

And they were singing Christmas carols.

Driving from the banks of the muddy Raritan—from the 400-person classes, from the bug-infested living areas, from the realization that every day for the next four years was going to be a lackluster one, to this, to Christmas carols, to the blind, unbothered, let's-get-together-and-belt-out-a-good-Silent-Night world of Princeton—pushed a button inside all three of us. Andy, Jeff, and I all froze, our seething resentment mixing with our collective self-loathing into a dangerously combustible mixture. This wasn't just cheesy. This wasn't just white bread in a way that would never survive at Rutgers. This was a rallying call to war. We were three kids who existed in a place where we found it hard to feel good about anything. We were three kids who woke up every day a little pissed off about how things were going. Most of all, we were three kids who spent so much time uncertain and angry that we were scared about whether we were going to turn out okay.

And there's no way you sit around singing Christmas carols unless you feel fine about the world. You have to be happy to sing a carol. That's why it's not just called a song. Just look in the dictionary:

'Car·ol [kar-*uhl*] *noun, verb*—oled, oling, olled, olling
1. a song, *especially of joy*

We were *real* Jersey kids, from a *real* place, with *real* problems. We certainly didn't stand around at night singing songs *of joy*. Sure, we were spoiled college kids too, but this was taking things to an entirely different level. These Princeton kids lived in a fantasy world where there were very few problems, and inexplicably, this fairy-tale place was sitting right in the middle of *our* state. Suddenly, without saying a word, all three of us knew we were going to do our damnedest to destroy that fantasy world.

Meanwhile, the kids around the piano, in what we noticed was becoming a trend, didn't blink twice at the three shady kids dressed in all black lurking around.

We made our way toward Rob and Derek's floor, heading up a stairwell, where we were again thwarted by the presence of a heavy door sealed shut with a magnetic lock. We banged on the door, and as each second ticked by, I realized what a bad idea it was to have come here. *This is a bad idea*, I thought to myself, *that I am about to do.* I mean, we were definitely going over-board. We were definitely worked up. And it really wasn't fair to direct it all at one unsuspecting kid. . . .

Just as we were coming to our senses, someone opened the door.

The kid was pudgy—that was the first thing you had to notice about him. Pudgy in a way that belied his innocence. Pudgy like veal, kept in a cage for its whole life so that experience wouldn't harden its muscles. His large eyes blinked behind his glasses, as if he had been sitting in darkness and we were beams of light. It was almost as if this level of human contact was jarring to him.

"Can I help you with something?" he asked. His voice was as soft and doughy as his childlike cheeks.

"We're friends of Rob's," I mumbled, rocking back and forth on my feet. He looked back at me, confused. "From Rutgers. We called him—he's, uh, not around. He told us we should wait for him until he gets back," I said.

He eyed me up and down. I couldn't tell if it was with suspicion or disdain.

"Well, you can wait with me, I guess," he said, obviously bothered that he'd have to babysit us. He motioned for us to follow him down the hallway. Over his shoulder, he off-handedly signed his own death warrant with three innocuous words: "My name's Deh-reek."

To Derek, Framsky was just a made-up name on the computer screen of some dude he lived down the hall from. He didn't know Framsky went to Rutgers. He didn't know how unhappy Framsky was with the way things were going for him. He wasn't aware of Framsky's habit of overreacting to small things, of making them out to be symbolic of how his entire life was going. He didn't know how angry he had made Framsky on that night.

Most importantly, he had no idea Framsky was the clad-in-black, skinny weirdo furiously staring at the back of his head right at that moment.

Derek almost seemed tragic to me then, completely oblivious to the level of fear to which he was going to be introduced that night. I started to feel bad. It was like standing on a hill, watching an unsuspecting car about to be blindsided by a speeding truck.

With those feelings rising, I knew that if I was going to bail, if I was going to forgive him and walk away, it would have to happen now.

Instead, I followed him into his dorm. Without turning around, he said, "There's some people drinking down the hall. I *guess* you can come."

When we got to the room in question there were about ten kids spread out with their backs to us, all laughing and drinking. Derek announced us. "Guys, these are Rob's friends from Rutgers," he said.

Without even turning to look at us, one of the young ladies said, "Oh, I thought something smelled funny in here all of a sudden."

She said it quickly, so quickly that it almost seemed planned. Even more quickly than Andy had answered, yes, he wanted to beat up a Princeton kid. But while I had admired that kind of quickness in Andy, I was aghast when I encountered it in that dorm room.

Who behaves that way? Were they sitting around all night waiting for some poor Scarlet Knight to walk through the door just so they could get that killer dig out? No—it wasn't pre-planned. These goddamned smart kids just knew how to think fast and articulate their thoughts. Before the insult, the entire night could have taken a turn right there. We could have sat and drank with those kids all night, burying our stereotypes of each other and uniting in the common bonding of being young and drunk. Instead, we were insulted the second we walked into the room.

At this point, it wasn't just me who was angry. Andy and Jeff were mad as well. They had entered that night as my backup on a silly adventure. Now, they had witnessed college kids singing Christmas carols around their grand piano on a Friday night, and had been insulted outright by a very smart, likely very rich girl. I, personally, was unhinged on a day-to-day basis, and not really of right mind. Admittedly, Andy fit that bill as well. But now even Jeff, who was the most straight-laced, together guy I knew, was pissed.

Still, my feelings toward Derek were becoming confused. I was angry about what he had done to me. But in a way I also pitied him: he had initially represented big bad Princeton in our minds, but I knew it wasn't right to take it all out on one guy. At the end of the day, I knew nothing about him. For all I knew, he could have been the me of Princeton—the token sad kid.

Noting his dorm-mate's clear displeasure that we had entered her room, Derek spun on his heels and led us back out into the hallway. We went down to the other end of the hall and followed him into what he explained was his own room. It was huge, at least three times the size of the space I shared with the Russian Bear.

"You guys can have a seat on the floor," he said.

I watched as he sat in an expensive-looking leather office chair, and my recently softened feelings toward him instantly rehardened. There were about six open chairs in his room, not to mention a small couch. But we had been invited to sit on the floor. I now knew everything I needed to know about Derek. He was nothing like me—he was the type of person who thinks it's okay to tell a stranger to sit on the floor.

"Actually, Derek," I said in a voice as calm as could be, "I'm going to sit wherever the fuck I want."

His head dropped, and he slowly turned around. He suddenly had the body language of someone who realized he was in some pretty deep shit—the type of deep shit where you invite a stranger over, disrespect him before your peers, ridicule him in private, and then realize you know nothing about him.

"I—," he hesitated. "I'm sorry, I never got your name."

I paused and locked eyes with him. I held the stare long enough to silently confirm his suspicions that he had fucked up pretty bad. I took a deep breath.

"My name's Framsky."

All color drained from his pudgy face, and everything about him suddenly screamed *I want to be back in Toronto right now.*

He tried his best not to let us sense the fear that was washing over his body.

"And your friends?" he asked. "What are their names?"

He sounded like he thought this was a game, like he was delivering his lines as some sort of mastermind. As if we were kids, playing, and he was filling the role of the bad guy. But I wasn't playing a game. I was lonely. I was socially depraved. I was depressed and scared about my life.

I snapped.

"THEIR NAME IS FRAMSKY TOO, MOTHERFUCKER!" I bellowed. I leaned in close to him. "DON'T YOU EVER FUCK WITH ME AGAIN."

All the rage that had slowly been building throughout my everyday life boiled over with the massive amount of disrespect I'd been handed since arriving at this dorm. My voice was aggressive.

I was lashing out, attacking, trying to beat Derek down verbally. And it was working. He was scared. But I was scared too—because I could feel in my gut that his being frightened was not enough for me. I felt my hands balling up into fists, and I was aware that I very much wanted to hit him.

"You have to go," Derek stammered. "You have to go right now." I ignored him.

"Don't you ever fuck with me," I reiterated. "You have no idea what it's like out there—you have no idea who I am."

From the look in his eyes, I knew something totally validating was happening. He was in the process of realizing that I was right. He didn't have any idea what it was like out there. He had as much of an idea about what my New Jersey was as I did about his. We were both freshmen in college, both the same age, and we lived thirty miles apart, but we couldn't have been more different if we had been born on different planets. We lived on two different planes of reality—socially, academically, and culturally. Tonight, those very different existences hit each other head-on, and it wasn't going well for Derek.

Tears welled up in his eyes. And that's when I spread out my arms, like a flying bird of prey, and said what might be the toughest thing I have ever said.

"I am in your house, motherfucker." I grinned. "I am in your fucking house. And there's nothing you can do about it."

He looked at me, and the first tear trickled down his cheek. I was taken aback. Only at a place like Princeton could a guy who looks like me be the bully instead of the bullied.

"You have to go, right now," he said, taking a step toward me.

"I am in your house," I repeated.

"Go. Leave," he said, trying desperately to control his fear.

"I am in your house," I said, borderline laughing in his face.

At this point I was completely lost in a maniacal rage. He took one more step and he pushed me. That was a mistake. I spun around.

"Framsky," I said matter-of-factly, making eye contact with Jeff, "shut the door."

"We need to leave," Jeff answered. I looked at him. He was no longer angry. He was scared. Of me. I looked from Jeff to Andy.

"Yeah," Andy said. "We need to leave right now."

～～～

We sprinted, nearly knocking each other over in an effort to get down the stairs. We ran back across campus, leaving behind the pristine dorms, grand pianos, and one fat crying Canadian with a very bright future. Back at Rutgers, Andy and Jeff hung out in my room for the rest of the night. We assumed the police were going to arrive at any moment and that our gathering in one place was a polite way to make their job easier. I don't know what I was more scared of—my impending arrest or the behavior I had seen in myself that night. I'd always been an angry kid, but usually it was directed inward and reflected itself in my cripplingly low self-esteem. For the first time, I'd gotten truly out of control and saw that anger lash outward. I'd almost brutalized a stranger. Worst of all, I wasn't sure which I felt worse about: almost doing it or not doing it.

To our amazement, the police never called.

～～～

"Did you know him?" my mother asked me years later, when I told her the story.

"No, he was a stranger. He messed with me on the Internet," I replied. She sighed. Even over the phone, I could sense her shaking her head at me.

"You went to Princeton to beat up a person you didn't know?" she asked with exasperation. I could hear the silent follow-up question that went unspoken—*What went wrong when I raised you?*

"Yeah. I never told you about that?"

"No, that's one of the things you never told me about," she said. "I never know what you're gonna come up with." Then I heard her quietly giggle, like any Jersey girl would at the thought of someone tormenting a Princeton Tiger.

"So what's new with you?" I asked her.

"Not much," she said. "I tried to send some people an email picture of a kitten, but it didn't work. . . . Have you ever heard of something like that?" She paused, and then said with a very heavy sigh, "Only me."

It was then that I remembered where my fatalistic penchant for melodrama came from.

~~~

Two years after my mission to Princeton, I went back for the first time. I had to be in the area anyway, so I gave Rob a call. He invited me to meet up so we could get dinner together. As we crossed the still bucolic Princeton campus, he pointed to a dorm.

"Do you remember that kid Derek?" he asked.

"How could I ever forget?"

"You know," he said, laughing to himself, "he lives in *that* dorm now."

"Really?"

"Yeah, actually in that corner," he said, "on the ground floor." Well, I had to.

I walked over to the window. It was late spring and unseasonably hot, so Derek's window was open, with only a screen covering the frame. Again utilizing my God-given abilities as a born-and-raised Jersey guy, I jimmied open the screen and stuck my head in.

Derek was there on his bed, sleeping in his tightie whities on his back. An oscillating fan was pointed toward him. It was so peaceful, it was almost cute. I leaned farther in.

"Derek!" I whispered, harshly.

He shot up out of bed and reached to the windowsill for his glasses. He fumbled with them for a moment, then put them on and looked my way.

It was two full years later, but to my satisfaction, his jaw dropped open.

"Framsky?" he said.

"I'm always watching, man," I said. "So you be good, Derek. You be good."

White Magic

If you asked me or my brother at the age of nine what we wanted to be when we grew up, we would have lied. We would have answered "police officer" or "teacher" or "astronaut." Those are the things you expect kids to say, and we knew that. We would never have publicly revealed our real dream, because our parents had made it very clear to us that our dream was embarrassing.

What we wanted to be were pro wrestlers. It didn't matter that both of us were the smallest kid in our respective classes. Gregg's braces and lazy eye? No problem. My deformed elbows and knobby knees? Pay them no mind. No matter what, we had to be professional wrestlers. It was the dream. Nothing could stand in our way, not even our father, who did everything he could to crush that dream without mercy or remorse.

"I just don't understand why you like that bullshit," he'd say, shaking his head. "Bullshit" was his description of choice when it came to wrestling, and it always made me furious. Then again, my father had good reason to hate the "sport."

Growing up, Gregg and I often imagined our yard was a wrestling ring. Once, when I was in fourth grade, we were staging a match that ended when I emulated wrestling superstar Sting's finisher, the "Stinger Splash," and came down unintentionally hard on my brother's chest.

"Stop working stiff, asshole," he shouted. He leapt to his feet and jumped into the air. His knee crashed into my shoulder, breaking it in two. I screamed and collapsed.

My mother appeared at the front door and saw me on the ground.

"What's the matter?" she asked.

"My shoulder," I sobbed. "It's broken."

"It is not," she said. "Stop being a baby. Now come inside and eat your dinner."

For the rest of the day, even though my collarbone jutted awkwardly beneath my skin, my parents refused to believe I'd broken anything. That night we attended a Super Bowl party, where Gregg and I got into another fight. Only when I couldn't swing with my left did my parents realize I was actually hurt and took me to the hospital. My brother and I were so consistently violent that it took my inability to produce more violence to prove to them something was wrong.

After that, my father forbade wrestling. Gregg and I had to sneak around to watch wrestling, turning the volume low and quickly changing the channel if my parents entered the room. It was our own personal taste of what it must have been like to live under Stalin, if Stalin had hated pro wrestling instead of dissidents and organized religion. (The comparison may seem like a stretch, but my dad does sport a very Stalinish moustache.)

And like dreams of democracy behind the Iron Curtain, my dream of being a professional wrestler remained hidden and suppressed, but never completely died. And one night when I was a freshman in college, for a brief, flashing moment I lived my dream. I broke through twelve years of secret obsession and came face-to-face with my ultimate destiny. For one night, I was no longer Chris Gethard, resident geek. For one night, I was White Magic.

Mere weeks into my tenure at Rutgers, the phone in my dorm room rang. It was an old friend of mine, another huge wrestling fan, Eddie.

"Dude, did I tell you I trained at Gino Caruso's wrestling school?" he asked.

"Yeah, I heard something about that," I told him. "How'd it go?"

"I was a terrible wrestler," he confided in me. "But I made a lot of connections." He paused, allowing the tension to build. "One of those connections is an agoraphobic man named Carmine," he said. It was the last thing I expected to hear.

"Like he's scared to leave his house?" I asked.

"The guy's scared of everything. But he's got boatloads of money," Eddie said.

"Okay," I said. "So what's this got to do with me?"

"Carmine is the owner of Stars and Stripes Championship Wrestling," Eddie explained. "He made me the promoter."

"Okay," I said, still unsure of where this was going.

"I want you to come be a manager on our next card," Eddie said.

Instantly, I was standing. A rush of euphoria overtook me and almost made me faint. I braced myself against my dresser and took a breath.

"Are you serious?" I asked. "This isn't some kind of joke?"

"No, dude," Eddie said, "we're living the dream."

Eddie knew I was a funny guy. He thought I had the chops to pull off the part and had convinced the agoraphobe owner of a wrestling league to grant me a job interview.

"This is amazing," I gushed.

"Come up with a character," he instructed, "and I'll call you back around seven tomorrow night. I'll be on three-way with Carmine."

I spent the evening cycling through some of the alter egos I'd created during my youth. There was no way I could pull off my two favorites—the Japanimal and the Haitian Sensation—due to the obvious racial implications. I had to leave my childhood wrestling fantasies behind as I made the transition to my adult wrestling reality. By evening's end, I'd come up with the most despicable persona I could muster: White Magic, an arrogant pimp dressed in a smoking jacket and top hat who would tout his money and girls to the very working-class wrestling fans he was paid to incite and degrade.

Standing in front of my mirror, I took a quick assessment of myself. I weighed 135 pounds. I was pale, and had huge glasses and a bowl haircut. White Magic would be everything I wasn't: smooth, a ladies' man, cocky, and quick with an insult. This was the first chance I'd ever had to redesign myself, and my instincts led me to instantly embrace a character that was in every way my opposite. After all, the dream of being a professional wrestler had never just been about professional wrestling; it was more about having the traits wrestlers had that I didn't—strength, re-siliency, and the ability to wear who you are on your sleeve.

By seven fifteen the call still hadn't come, and I began to feel the sinking sensation of despair. I was heartbroken. Maybe Eddie had overstated his influence with the owner, maybe he was just playing a prank. Maybe the agoraphobic was in a particularly fearful mood and couldn't even manage to talk that day.

Just as I was about to give up hope, the phone rang.

"Hello?" I answered, trying not to sound too eager.

"Chris," Eddie said, "I'm on the line with Carmine."

"Hi, Carmine," I said.

"Hi," he said, tersely. "Real nice to meet you." He sounded terrified.

"Thanks for this opportunity," I said. "This would really be a dream come true."

"Why don't you tell me about your character?" he said.

"I'll call myself White Magic," I began. "A smooth-talking showoff pimp."

I could tell the gears in Carmine's head were already turning.

"Could you tell me a little bit about what you look like?" he asked. He had the cadence of an early-era Marlon Brando, if Brando had spent his entire life indoors and was convinced that the world was out to get him.

"Well," I began, "I weigh 135 pounds. I have glasses—"

"Say no more, my friend," Carmine interrupted. "I can see how that would get a crowd real hot. Why don't we do some role-play?"

"Excuse me?" I asked.

"WHITE MAGIC! You sorry son of a bitch," he began. "Where do you get off coming 'round these parts?"

I was thrown, but recovered and dove into character.

"White Magic come 'round any parts he wants," I told him. "'Cause I got hos in ALL THE ZIP CODES!"

"Well, you need to step off—'cause around here, nobody messes with me," Carmine bellowed. For an agoraphobic, he was turning out to be awfully aggressive.

"Nobody messes with you? I mess with who I want," I yelled at him. "Yo momma. Yo momma's momma. Even yo baby daughta if I feel like it. I'm White Magic, baby—casting pimp spells and raising pimp hell!"

Carmine didn't answer. After a pause, I heard him giggle and I knew I was in.

He explained that there was an event being held that Saturday in an auditorium at Seton Hall University in South Orange. I'd be managing a man named Vicious Vin who, like me, would be participating in his first match ever. He was scheduled to go up against a local indie wrestler named Flash Wheeler, who had been around for a while. I had a few days to get an outfit together and come up with a routine that would get the crowd to absolutely hate me.

As luck would have it, I happened to have a top hat that I previously wore to my junior prom (I was *that* guy). My friend Andy had a Hugh Hefner–style smoking jacket, because he was a classy dresser with an appreciation for the finer things in life. Down the hall lived John, a fellow wrestling fanatic and a graphic designer. He took a white T-shirt and painted the words "White Magic" on it in an obnoxious font. Inside the pocket of the shirt I pinned two Phillies Blunt cigars. The master touch was a mahogany cane. I looked in the mirror and realized that I fit the part. I was on the precipice of living my dream. I was giddy, nervous, and overwhelmed. I needed support, but this situation was ludicrous. My next step was to call the one person I absolutely knew would back me up.

"Gregg?" I asked when my brother picked up. "Are you sitting down?"

"Yeah," he answered. "Is everything all right?"

"I'm going to be a manager in a pro wrestling league on Saturday," I told him.

He paused.

"I'll be there," he said. "I've never been more proud of you in my life."

I glanced back at the mirror. I was fired up. I was dressed correctly. I was ready.

I was White Magic.

On the day of the event, a handful of people I knew came to watch. My brother was there to witness a dream fulfilled, sitting next to my girlfriend Veronica. John came to see how the outfit he designed played to the crowd. All of them knew how much this meant to me.

Before I left them to get ready, my brother turned to me. "Dude, you're in," he said. "Make it happen."

"Thanks, man," I said.

My girlfriend said nothing. At the time, I assumed it must have been because she was overwhelmed with pride. I was too young to realize it was probably shame.

Eddie was in a cordoned-off corner littered with equipment, going over the lighting design with a handful of technicians.

"Eddie," I said as I approached. "Thanks for having me, man."

"It's gonna be great," Eddie said. "I'm glad I get to be here for your debut."

He directed me to the changing area, which actually wasn't even a room—just a corner of the auditorium partitioned off with a large freestanding wall and a number of attached curtains. There, I met "the boys."

As I entered, I was struck with an overwhelming dose of reality; this was really happening. It was the culmination of every childhood fantasy I'd ever had. Even if it had been your average low-rent local wrestling card it would have been emotional. But this introduction was particularly awe-inspiring. In addition to the local wrestlers, there were some bona fide wrestling legends present.

The massive, bald-headed King Kong Bundy, a villain I had watched since my youth, sat in one corner. Marty Jannetty of the Rockers walked in behind me, and former WWF world champion The Iron Sheik made his entrance a few minutes later, already wearing his curlicue-toed boots when he got there. ECW wrestler Skull Von Krush, whose gimmick was that he was a neo-Nazi, sat talking with Ring of Honor standout Low Ki.

I stared out at the arena. It was nothing special—just a multi-purpose room with a wrestling ring set up in the middle and a hundred folding chairs around it. It was the equivalent of going to see a Single A minor league baseball game. But to me, with my idols present and a lifetime of fantasies coming to fruition, it was the big time.

Eddie grabbed my arm and pulled me out of my daze. He directed me to a corner where Flash Wheeler and Vicious Vin were discussing the mechanics of our match.

"For the storyline we're building," Eddie told me, "we need Vin to win."

"Okay," I said.

"Since Vin clearly doesn't have the chops Flash has, we need to figure out a way that the crowd will buy it," Eddie continued.

"Makes sense," I responded.

"And that's where you come in."

Eddie informed me that I would use my cane to bash Flash Wheeler over the head. This underhanded cheating would allow Vicious Vin to pin the more experienced wrestler without the crowd questioning the outcome. My mouth went dry. I was under the impression my job was to get people riled up, not to get physically involved in the match.

Flash grabbed me and sat me down. His muscular hand wrapped around my entire bicep, and when I looked into his eyes I saw the empty expanse of a man with no morals. "Listen the fuck up," he said. "I'll spin my finger in a circle and bounce off the ropes."

"Okay," I said.

"When I do, you jump up," he barked. "Hit me with that cane. I'll go down. Then I'll let fucking fat ass pin me." He motioned to Vin, who looked as intimidated as I felt.

As soon as Eddie walked away, Flash Wheeler turned to me again.

"I don't know what you're doing here," he said, staring me dead in the eye. "You have no training. You've put no time in to deserve being here." He paused to make sure I was paying attention. Needless to say, I was. "And if you hit me with that cane the wrong way and injure me," he continued, "I am going to fuck you up."

I was terrified. Before I had time to digest his words, someone grabbed me and pushed me toward the curtains. It was time for my dream to finally come true.

I strutted out with my top hat and cane, and got the exact reaction I was hoping for. The sight of a nerdy kid acting like a high-status lothario immediately drew ire from the angry mob. Thanks to their reaction I snapped out of my Flash Wheeler–induced fear and came to life. Insulting white-trash wrestling fans came naturally to me—as naturally as anything ever has. I was in the heart of North Jersey, just a town away from where I grew up. The fans who showed up that night were obnoxious locals who reminded me of the bullies I knew as a kid. Being encouraged to insult them was permission to take out all the aggression that lived inside me.

"You can't be a pimp," one man in the first row shouted at me. His kids laughed as he pointed at me. "To be a pimp, you actually have to talk to a girl once in a while."

I sprinted over to the railing in front of his seats.

"Shut up, idiot!" I shouted at him. "I don't want to have to slap your mouth in front of your daughter." I said it loud enough for everyone to hear. "Anything else you want to say?" I said, raising my arms and leaning in close to him. He didn't answer.

The crowd loudly jeered. I was a villain in their eyes. I *was* White Magic.

Another guy pointed at me. Just as he was about to yell something, I cut him off. "Old man," I said, in a tone loud enough to get him to freeze in his tracks. "Sit the fuck down before I come over there and smack those last two hairs off your ugly bald head!"

I climbed into the ring and strutted around. The verbal sparring continued. I had them in the palm of my hand. I was controlling their emotions. I was exhilarated by the level of control I was able to wield while inciting such chaos. When the bell rang, I rolled out under the ropes and continued jawing with spectators as the match got under way.

I watched Vicious Vin and Flash go at it. As someone who has seen thousands of wrestling matches, I knew it was bad. Vin was confused. His movements were halting and unconfident. Flash's irritation at the plummeting quality of his match led to overaggression, and that only exacerbated the problem. He was throwing his shots harder and wilder. It scared me, knowing that I'd soon have to jump in and contribute.

All I could think about were Flash Wheeler's words of warning. I was getting cold sweats. Despite my success at riling the crowd, I knew Flash was completely correct. I had no right to be there. And my lack of training *could* hurt him. Vicious Vin's bad timing alone had Flash visibly infuriated, and he was hitting Vin with open-handed slaps that left red welts on the fat rookie wrestler. If I fucked up hitting him with a thick piece of wood, I could be in some serious shit.

The match flew by. And eventually, the signal came. Flash looked down at me and circled with his finger. He sprinted across the ring, bouncing off the ropes toward me.

This was it. A moment I'd dreamed about since I was five years old. The moment I became a wrestler. Up until then, I'd been a part of things, but really I'd been standing just outside a wrestling ring shouting insults while wearing a funny outfit. Now, I got to leap to the edge of the squared circle and participate. It was a coming-out ceremony for me, the fulfillment of a lifelong dream.

I froze.

Flash hit the ropes in front of me and nothing happened. He ran back in the other direction, and Vicious Vin made eye contact with me, making a distinct *What the fuck are you doing?* face. Flash bounced off the ropes and awkwardly came back in my direction, as if a single Irish whip from Vicious Vin was powerful enough to cause him to run back and forth three entire times without being able to stop himself.

I knew I had to fulfill my duties. I jumped up on the ring apron, raised my cane, and swung.

In that moment, I had the opportunity to act on any number of impulses.

I could have smashed the cane over Flash's head extra hard as retaliation for being a terrifying asshole to me earlier.

I could have used this act of violence to affirm that I had what it took to live this dream, no matter what my parents thought.

I could have searched out my brother in the crowd and hit Flash as a sign of solidarity between us.

I could have caught eyes with my girlfriend and hit him in an impressive display of masculinity.

If any of these impulses had run through my head I would have been grateful.

Because what actually went through my head was blinding fear and nothing but: both a general fear of having the spotlight on me and a specific fear of screwing up and having Flash Wheeler deliver his promised ass kicking afterward. That fear paralyzed me during my big moment, and it would be an understatement to say that I choked.

The hit I delivered to Flash Wheeler with my cane wouldn't have fazed a ninety-year-old man with brittle bone disease. Doctors slap babies harder than I hit Flash with my cane. Orchestra conductors tap their music stands harder than I hit him. I'm a natural weakling. So for me to not put any effort into it was a sham. I lightly grazed the top of his head with the cane and then immediately leapt off the ring apron.

To his credit, Flash sold the move. He fell down, holding his head, thrashing about as if he was in extreme pain. For a moment, I thought things had turned out all right.

Maybe people will believe, I thought to myself, *that my cane has some sort of magical powers. That within it are superhuman levels of strength, and the cane is powerful, even though I am a visible coward.*

Unfortunately, that didn't happen. The crowd laughed and booed me. They knew I botched the ending of the match. My mystique as a smart-mouthed asshole had been stripped away by my pitiful physical display. For a few fleeting minutes, I had lived my dream. Now, as that dream fell apart around me, I faced a tidal wave of scorn and disrespect.

A group of preteens jumped the railing, and one pushed me as hard as he could.

"Stop, kid!" I shouted.

"Who's gonna make me, faggot?" he yelled back at me. One of his friends snuck up behind me and stole my top hat.

Earlier I'd been quick with my verbal sparring. The best I could muster as this teenaged hooligan ran off with my hat was a meek "Hey! I need that!"

Someone grabbed my arm. I turned to see that it was a wrestler I hadn't been introduced to yet. In the melee, I had forgotten that there was supposed to be a brawl in the aisle after our match. I looked into his eyes and saw the unmistakable look of *Don't fuck this up too.* The unnamed wrestler whipped me back toward the dressing room.

I hit the freestanding wall that marked the border of the dressing room face-first. The impact forced the structure to wobble back and forth. It tipped toward me, then away from me, and finally fell toward the dressing area, dragging down curtains on the way and exposing a group of very shocked, partially dressed professional wrestlers.

The wall crashed to the ground six inches from King Kong Bundy. He looked down, then raised his bald head and made eye contact with me. Seeing the enraged, murder-hungry eyes of a professional wrestler six times my size filled me with an icy fear that has yet to and likely never will be equaled.

I had arrived to live out a childhood dream, to become a conquering hero who claimed my destiny while (as all heroes do) proving my father wrong. Instead, I came inches away from killing a 400-pound behemoth I'd been watching on TV for as long as I could remember, and who now wanted to unleash the very moves I once cheered for to destroy my scrawny body.

The staff hoisted the wall back up. Before it was fully righted, I ducked behind it. No one would even look at me. No one except for Skull Von Krush, who wandered over to where I was

cowering. I thought he was going to console me, to tell me everyone makes rookie mistakes.

"You almost killed Bundy!" the neo-Nazi shouted, holding
his face inches from mine. "If you had hurt Bundy, we woulda
fucked you up. Maybe we still should, huh?"

"Bundy's fine!" I squeaked. "He's out there wrestling his
match right now!"

It was to no avail. Von Krush stayed in my face. He was mad,
and he was not backing down. People gathered around to watch
the verbal beatdown. I was being laughed at by the wrestlers—a
group I'd come into the evening hoping to impress.

And then, mercifully, the fire alarm went off.

Everyone jumped up and ran to peek out of the curtains. I
stayed slumped in the corner.

"Bundy got slammed!" someone yelled. "He's so heavy, it set
off the fire alarm!"

The wrestlers panicked. The confused crowd slowly filtered
out of the auditorium. I slipped out the back door and ran to
my car. My brother was there waiting for me.

"I grabbed it from those kids," Gregg said, handing me my
top hat before patting me on the back. We sat silently, in a rare
moment only brothers who once fought until their bones were
broken can experience. We exchanged a look and understood
that the dream was over.

I learned a hard, valuable lesson that night: childhood fantasies should remain fantasies. In the end, wrestling did little
more for me in life than break my shoulder as a child and shatter
my ego as a young adult. I would never tear my clothing before
amazed audiences. I would never do backflips off the ring's
ropes. And while learning that meant I had to live through a
heartbreaking and humiliating night, in the end that would have

to be fine. At some point we all have to learn to live as who we are and not as who we wish we were.

~~~

My parents recently asked me to remove a bunch of belongings I had stored in their basement. I spent hours sifting through old junk and eventually stumbled upon a dusty cardboard box. Inside was my top hat. My face burned with humiliation as I remembered the last night I had worn it. I threw it on the garbage pile, then reconsidered. I kept it, if only to remind myself that some dreams should remain just that.

I was smart enough to never tell my dad this story. He would have just called it bullshit anyway.

He would have been right. I am not White Magic.

I Fought the Law and the
Law Most Definitely Won

I am not a stupid person. I graduated from a well-known (though overrated) college. I read *The Economist* (only on airplanes, but that still counts). I DVR *Meet the Press* (although I also DVR *America's Best Dance Crew*). What I'm saying is that I'm normally a fairly intelligent person who doesn't actively look for stupid situations to get involved in, or who revels in his own stupidity. I think that's what makes the depths of my occasional stupidity that much more profound.

For example, I once microwaved a plate and a metal fork, and didn't know this was a problem until a slowly rotating ball of flame erupted inside my appliance.

"Dude, what the fuck are you doing?" my roommate yelled as he opened the door and saw the microwave on fire. I was watching reruns of *Beverly Hills 90210*.

"Shut up, it's the season where Brandon's dating that racist girl," I answered.

I once drank an entire cup of pinto beans thinking it was some sort of soup. It was not soup. It was a cup of beans, companion to the rice I had previously consumed. I drank the liquid surrounding the beans from the cup directly, as if it were a broth. This was stupid both in that (a) I don't know the difference between beans and soup and (b) I don't use spoons.

Years ago I was walking with my friend Kevin on a hot day in Manhattan, when I made an observation that turned into yet another stunning display of my occasional idiocy.

"It seems like the city's always cooler than Jersey," I said. "I wonder why that is."

"Oh," he answered. "We have this law here. If you have an air conditioner facing into your apartment, you're required to have a second one facing out to cool the street."

"That," I answered, quite seriously, "is the smartest thing I've ever heard."

He stopped in shock. Disappointment washed over his face.

"I was kidding, you fucking fool," he said.

But at best, each of these examples is a distant runner-up to what I can easily say was the dumbest thing I've ever done. When I think of the incident in question, I try to make excuses. "I was young." "I was overtaxed mentally." "It's probably good for a man to go batshit nuts once every few years." None of these excuses hold water. Now, more than a decade after the incident occurred, I still can't fathom what got into me.

Of course, it had to do with a car.

〜〜〜

I've known my roommate for fifteen years.

"I've never been in a car with you," he recently told me, "without feeling like I was going to die."

I've long been convinced that when I meet my end it will in all likelihood be behind the wheel of a car. It's not that I'm a bad driver. I think I'm actually the most highly evolved driver on the road. One day everyone else will finally understand how I drive and eventually catch up. It's like when people say to athletes: "Oh you can't run that distance in that time." And then someone will do it and then, like, six other people will do it the next year and everyone will amend their comments to say, "Oh I guess it *is* possible after all. We can do that. Humanity has reached that point." That is how I drive. Eventually humanity will catch up and recognize me as a pioneer, as a trendsetter. Who likes to go fast. And doesn't really see the point in being cautious.

Every time I've ever sat down in a driver's seat and my mother is nearby, we go through the same routine. As I buckle up and adjust my mirrors, she solemnly walks to the driver's side of the car. I roll down my window and patiently look at her.

"Please," she pleads, making direct eye contact, "drive carefully."

I ignore this request.

A handful of amazing feats and daring accomplishments I have pulled off behind the wheel of a car that I am genuinely proud of include: driving from New Jersey to Chicago by myself without stopping for anything besides gas; a four-day stretch where if I wasn't sound asleep I was driving, and that includes eating all of my meals behind the wheel; driving cross-country by myself in three days; making it through traffic from the Jersey Shore to Manhattan during rush hour in under forty-five minutes, achieved through a combination of dangerous weaving, a commitment to never using the brakes, and self-motivation achieved by repeatedly shouting the words "I am the King of New Jersey!" at my terrified girlfriend.

All of these fall into that wonderful category of "either high points or very, very low points in life." The apex of these moments, the decision that to this day I still consider my stupidest, happened when I was twenty years old.

When I was a junior in college, Wednesdays were the stressful turning point of my week. I was taking a full course load of classes, but ambitiously decided that I could also work two full days a week forty-five minutes north of my school. I managed to pack five classes in from Monday to Wednesday, exhausting myself in the process. It was all worth it because of my job—I was the sole employee working side by side with the two owners of a magazine called *Weird NJ*, a journal dedicated to chronicling anything bizarre, haunted, or odd about New Jersey. I defy anyone to tell me of a cooler job they had in college.

The *Weird NJ* office was in my hometown of West Orange. While that was pretty far north of Rutgers, it was only a short drive from my parents' new house a few towns away. So each Wednesday, as I sat through night class desperately trying to stay awake, I knew that I had an hour's drive ahead of me. By driving home at night, I'd determined I could avoid rush-hour traffic in the morning, which would allow me to get an extra half hour of sleep. Living the kind of schedule I was, the phrase "getting an extra half hour of sleep" sounded as appealing as "walking free" sounds to a prisoner or "hooking up with the lady who plays Jane Holloway on *Mad Men*" sounds to the modern heterosexual male.

After my classes wrapped up a few minutes before ten, I'd give myself just enough time to grab a quick dinner; then I'd rush home and jump in the car.

I've always had a very good ability to rationalize things. During those late-night drives to my parents' house I'd often say things to myself such as "There's not too many other cars on the road tonight, I can cut loose a bit." Or "Since I'm so tired, it's a

responsible thing to drive really fast and get off the road sooner."
Or "It's necessary that I speed; I'm going to have to be well-rested
and at the top of my game if I am to fulfill my duty as a chroni-
cler of New Jersey's best ghost stories." Regardless of my ration-
alizations, the point is I drove way too fucking fast.

Of course, my behavior did have its consequences. By the
time I was twenty, I'd already gotten a handful of speeding tickets and crashed a couple cars. In each case, per the laws of the
state of New Jersey, I received points. Not good points, like in
basketball. Bad points, like in golf. I had eleven points. Twelve
points was when the state stepped in to say, "It would be safer
for literally everyone else if we took away your license for the
next three to five years."

That night, charging north on Route 287 going 80 in a 65
when I already had eleven points was already a dumb decision.
But then there's what came next.

While my dangerous proximity to the points-based driving
cutoff certainly doesn't excuse it, I do think it helps explain my
reaction when I saw the headlights of a car sitting on the highway's median blink on as I flew past. In the split second it took
for me to realize that the lights to my left could only belong to a
police officer, I knew my license was going to get suspended.
That's when I took a bad situation brought on by my own dumb
behavior and threw some dumb fuel on the dumb fire. I hit
the gas.

Without really thinking I intentionally initiated a high-speed
chase with a New Jersey state trooper.

"My mother is going to kill me," I mumbled as I pushed the
pedal to the floor.

By the time the cop turned completely onto the road, I was
driving well over 90 miles per hour and had put a considerable

amount of distance between us. Unfortunately, he was game for the challenge. I looked in my rearview. As he completed his turn, he squared his car directly behind me and began catching up very, very quickly.

Still, for some reason he didn't turn on his sirens or lights.

I guess that means I'm not doing anything wrong, I tried to convince myself. *If his lights aren't on. . . .*

He was gaining ground fast, but I was coming up on the next exit, which would dump me out in a sedate, rich town called Bernardsville. I knew from my time at *Weird NJ* that Bernardsville was home to the Devil's Tree, a freaky-looking tree that supposedly kills you if you touch it. More importantly, I knew that the town had a lot of desolate, dark roads. If I could just make it to the exit before the cop caught up to me, I figured, I might be able to kill some time on those dark roads and lose him for good.

I took the exit, slowing down only as much as inertia and gravity forced me to. It was a sprawling horseshoe exit that looped around wide before heading into town. As I screeched to a halt at the stop sign at the end of the exit ramp, I saw the cop speeding on to the far end of the horseshoe, still tailing me.

You can still stop, I thought to myself. *He'll probably take it easier on you if you just stop now. . . . Or, fuck it.*

I gunned it again.

For some reason, in my exhausted, anxiety-addled state, I'd begun to think of my behavior as somehow heroic. Like I was the little guy and the cop was "the man" who was "keeping me down." Like it was a battle of epic proportions and I had to "win." Meanwhile, from the perspective of anyone not living in the world inside my head, I was simply an asshole who was driving too fast and now attempting to evade arrest.

I made a left onto a wide, tree-lined street. Every time I had a chance to turn onto a narrower, more desolate-looking road, I took it. Then, as I came to the end of a cul-de-sac, I pulled off a driving feat that was badass even for me: a '70s cop show–style peelout. I hit the brakes and my car spun to a stop. The smell of burning rubber lingered in the air. For a person as tragically un-cool as I am, it was a pretty cool moment.

I turned off the car and threw myself to the floor. I formed my body into a tight ball and wedged myself between my seat and the car's pedals.

I breathed heavily as the adrenaline rushed through my body.

I did it, I thought to myself. *I got away.*

I sat up and peeked out the window, my thoughts racing a mile a minute.

If he comes down here, I can sprint through those woods, I told myself. *I bet there are tons of places to hide in there.*

But then, as the stillness of the air set in around me and I no-ticed how quiet it was—only crickets broke the silence—the euphoric feeling of escaping the cop quickly twisted and hard-ened into a pure terror that sank low into the pit of my stomach.

Holy shit, I thought to myself, *I just broke more laws in the last fifteen minutes than in the rest of my entire life.*

My adrenaline crashed and I went into a panic.

I understood that I'd fucked up really bad. I also knew that the cop was definitely still out there. It had been only a few min-utes; there was no way he had given up yet.

I'll never do something this stupid again, I thought to myself. I looked at the roof of my car and put in a quiet plea to God. *I swear. Just please don't let him find me.*

Sitting at the end of a dead-end street wasn't a good strategy. If he didn't come and find me personally, then someone in the neighborhood was definitely going to call the police on me. It was the middle of the night and I was sitting in my crappy car in a cul-de-sac, lurking in the darkness in a rich neighborhood. I couldn't just wait and pray that I would get out of there.

My only hope was to get back to the highway without running into the cop again. I turned the car on and headed back out into the neighborhood, making random turns on the crisscrossed streets. My hope was that if I picked an unexpected pattern of roads on the way out, he wouldn't be able to catch up to me, as if I were Pac-Man and he were one of the ghosts.

I managed to make it back out to the main road without the cop finding me. I headed to the highway, and soon the on-ramp was in sight. For a fleeting moment I thought I was going to make it.

Not surprisingly, the cop turned out to be much smarter than I was. As I passed a hidden driveway just a few hundred feet away from the highway entrance, a set of headlights blinked on. This time, I tried proving that I'd learned from my mistake by pulling over immediately.

The cop pulled up behind me and directed his spotlight into my rearview mirror, blinding me. Though I couldn't see anything, I heard him get out of his car. He slammed his door angrily and made his way toward me. He shined his flashlight into my side-view mirror in a successful effort to blind me just a little bit more.

"License, registration, insurance now!" he barked at me.

"Sir, I'm really sorry," I said. In my experience with cops, the only way to get out of a ticket was to be completely subservient. "I—"

"SHUT UP," he screamed at me, red in the face.

I opened my wallet and handed him my license. Then I meekly opened my glove compartment to get the rest of my paperwork, and grimaced when I realized things were about to get much, much worse.

"Sir, I hate to say this, but I seem to not have my registration and insurance cards on me right now," I squeaked.

"Are you kidding me?" he asked, genuinely baffled. This hard-nosed, no-nonsense police officer honestly thought I was messing with him.

"No, sir," I said. "I seem to have misplaced them." I looked at him, doing my best to convey the demeanor of a remorseful and cowardly man, hoping he'd take pity on me. He looked over my license.

"Where are you headed, Mr. Get Hard?" he asked. I didn't correct his pronunciation.

"Home," I answered.

"Back to Fairfield?" His tone made it clear that this was another nail in the coffin.

"Yes, sir," I said.

"Well, then," he grunted, "this exit is not on the way to Fairfield. I guess it's safe to surmise that the only reason you got off at this exit was to evade capture by me."

I was done trying to get away. I hadn't managed to drive my way out of this mess, and there was definitely no way I was going to talk my way out of it either. I mentally prepared myself for a night in prison.

"Yes, sir, that's correct," I replied. He shook his head before turning back toward his car. Before he walked away, I blurted out exactly what was on my mind.

"And I just want to say that this is easily the stupidest thing I've ever done in my entire life."

I didn't say it in a whiny or pleading voice. My tone was flat. I just wanted it on the record. I fucked up, and for some reason, I wanted to make sure he knew I knew that.

He looked at me with a combination of hatred and confusion. "Yes," he said. "Yes, it is."

He walked toward his car, his boots clicking on the asphalt. My heart raced as I thought of what life would be like now that my driving privileges would be replaced with a criminal record. Then, the officer paused. He turned and headed back in my direction. I braced myself for a tongue-lashing. Instead, he reached toward the window.

"Get home safe, Christopher," he muttered, handing me back my license.

"Oh. Okay," I said.

I leaned out the window as he turned and walked away.

"I'm really sorry to have wasted your time tonight, sir," I said.

He didn't answer. He got into his car and disappeared onto the highway. I shook, unable to process that he had actually let me go. Anxiety overtook me along with an overpowering sinking feeling. Now that I was out of trouble, I retroactively experienced all of the fear and nervousness that should have stopped me from going on such an ill-advised adventure in the first place. For a moment, I honestly thought I was going to shit my pants.

Luckily I managed to calm down before evacuating my bowels. Driving home, I thought about how dumb I had been. I thought about how my schedule was crazy, how I was slowly killing myself—mentally if not physically—and how things needed to change.

I was also left with one nagging question: Why did he let me go? Maybe he appreciated the honesty I put on display through my admission of guilt and subsequent condemnation of my own intelligence. Maybe I just got lucky, and pulling off the highway meant I had left his jurisdiction, that all he *could* do legally was put the fear of God in me. Maybe I was so visibly pathetic that he decided to take pity. I will never know the answer, but I spent a lot of time thinking about it both as I drove home that night and since.

Despite my fear, I also thought about how many (yes, ill-advised but absolutely and undeniably) badass things I had pulled off that night.

I'm glad the cop didn't give me a ticket. But not just because I avoided the points and retained my license. All the tickets up to that point hadn't had an effect on me. I'd viewed avoiding them as some sort of weird self-destructive game. In my mind, I had every right to behave how I wanted. It was the cops' job to try and stop me and it was my job to try and get away. We were all just playing our roles.

That cop's leniency was a choice. It made me realize that I had choices, too. I could choose to not push things so far. I could choose to live a less hectic life that wouldn't make me feel that behaving like an insane asshole lunatic was either necessary or cool. I could choose to take care of myself, to put my health and safety ahead of my ambitions and obsessions. Most importantly, in a few different ways, I could choose to slow down.

Eventually I did. But I'm still a driving prodigy, and one day you and everyone else will see the way.

Nemesis

As a tried-and-true nerd, I've always suspected that finding one's nemesis was just another step in the process of becoming a man. You grow hair on your body, your voice changes, and you find your ideological counterpart to stand in stark juxtaposition to, highlighting your own heroic tendencies in the process.

Spider-Man had the Green Goblin. Hulk Hogan had King Kong Bundy. And I had Nick Forman. As with nearly every other aspect of puberty, I didn't discover my nemesis until I was in college.

I didn't learn much of anything during my time at Rutgers. I was an American Studies major. I signed up for it because my only goal was to graduate while doing as little work as possible. American Studies was great because most of the class titles could conceivably end in an exclamation point. "Urban Adventure!," "P.T. Barnum!," and "Murder in America!" were just a few of the notables from my transcript.

One summer class I took was titled "The Cowboy in Fiction and Film!" We watched a movie during each class, one of them being *Shanghai Noon* starring Owen Wilson and Jackie Chan. I didn't read any of the books. Each week I'd put my head down and fall sound asleep immediately once class began.

But one day a discussion about a book titled *The Virginian* was keeping me awake. The professor was describing a scene involving a chicken sitting on a rock after its egg had been taken from its nest. He asked the class about the symbolism behind the chicken's behavior. I hadn't read the book, but the conversation was annoying enough to interrupt my slumber, so I took action.

"Chris?" the professor asked when I raised my hand. It's always a sign that you've slacked off when a teacher calls on you in question form.

"Yeah," I said, wiping sleep from my eyes. "Here's the thing. Even though it was just a chicken it lived life and, therefore, had dreams. That egg represented its dreams."

Everyone stared at me. For the majority, it was the first time they had heard me speak.

"When the egg was taken away, the chicken sat on a rock," I continued. "Why? Because even though it knew its dreams wouldn't come true, it still had to chase them."

I squinted and melodramatically gazed out the window.

"It's something all of us would be well served to learn," I said. "Achieving your dreams is not always the most important part of life; *having* dreams is."

"Exactly," the professor said. He smiled at me.

With that, I dropped my head down on my desk and fell right back asleep.

The only downside to my major was that it required me to take two real classes through the history department. I took mine with a feisty Southern professor named George Kayne. To this day, he's the only person I've ever seen manage to look tough while wearing a sweater vest.

"If you ever have to take a history class," my friend Sean Gorman told me at the beginning of freshman year, "take it with George Kayne."

"Why?" I asked. "Is he easy?"

"No, he's hard," Sean said. "But he's insane . . . in an entertaining way."

Legend had it that Kayne used to be the chair of the department, but got demoted for punching another professor in the face. He would stalk around the room shouting like a bulldog and turning red in the face. I once watched him make a girl cry on the first day of class for no reason. He even laughed as she exited the room.

"Your tears mean nothing to me!" he exclaimed as she fled.

With such a badass at the helm, you'd think I would have shaped up. But I remained a slacker. Due in part to a nasty addiction to *Mike Tyson's Punch Out* on Nintendo, I managed to screw myself for finals week and had to scramble to get all of my work done. I'd lost the syllabus for Kayne's class and was forced to email him the day before a paper was due. Out of fear, I used a fake email address—cgdupree@hotmail.com.

"Hey Professor Kayne!" I began. "It's CG Dupree from your Monday/Wednesday class. I'm psyched to get crackin' on this paper, but I just realized I lost the topic. If you could email me back with it, I'd really appreciate it. Thanks!"

I woke the next morning to an email from Kayne in CG Dupree's inbox.

"Dear whoever you are," it read. "There is no one registered in my class under the name CG Dupree. Furthermore, anyone who would start a paper of mine with less than a day to go is destined to fail—not just the paper, but at life in general."

School wasn't doing it for me, and the more I drifted away from having any sense of academic standards, the more I felt like

I had no place there. In movies about the college experience, the slackers and outcasts find each other. They live together, bonding over their own idiosyncrasies and turning them into their greatest strengths. The helpless freshmen in *Animal House* learn to idolize Bluto. The Lambda Lambda Lambdas form their own frat, boxing out the rest of the Greek system. I wanted to find my own band of brothers to embrace my outside nature with, to unite together against the mainstream. And for a brief window in time, I thought I did.

My sophomore year I moved into a house with five other guys, each one of them a social misfit. Mark was an aspiring rapper who lost his mind freshman year and dropped fifty pounds just to see if he could. Anthony literally never stopped playing video games. The only break he'd give himself was to attend his Chinese calligraphy course. Jesse wore a trench coat—as he had all through high school—despite the fact that Columbine had happened just six months before we moved into our house. His refusal to alter his fashion in reaction to Columbine only made him seem more Columbineish. Eric was a lovable Taiwanese goofball who had never drunk alcohol before living with us. Within weeks of shared residency, he'd become a champion booze-bag and was piously dedicated to online poker.

Over the course of one painfully long year, our house became a pressure cooker that would drive each of us to the brink of madness. The first sign of impending disaster was an infestation of camel crickets—bugs so big and terrifying we once crushed one with a dictionary and flushed it down the toilet only to watch it climb back out. If I had to give you a proper description, I would say a camel cricket is basically a cross between a grasshopper and a dragon and that its natural habitat is the nightmares of men.

In addition, our house was robbed multiple times. We figured the person robbing us was the man who we routinely caught staring into our basement windows, but the crack patrol down at the New Brunswick PD told us that this wasn't enough of a lead to go on.

Without question, the place was a hellhole. But it was also just bizarre. For example, a radiator was mounted on the ceiling directly above Anthony's bed. There was also a hole in the floor directly next to where he slept. We'd drop items down into it and never hear them land. Anthony developed insomnia caused by the knowledge that even if he somehow managed to dodge the radiator that could fall onto him at any moment, he would likely plunge into a bottomless pit in the process.

The list of insanities went on and on. A bat attacked me in my bedroom. The toilets often clogged and my roommates were inconsiderate—a deadly combination that eventually led to a toilet explosion that ended with me crying in the shower, desperately trying to scrub my legs clean of the drunken diarrhea Eric had left behind. It was enough to question the value of our society, let alone our education system.

It's fair to say that in the face of such madness and atrocity, my final roommate, Nick Forman, was actually the one who was able to hold it together the best. At least up to a point. When Nick broke it wasn't the living in filth that got him. It wasn't being attacked by insects from another planet.

In the end what destroyed Nick Forman was the movie *Fight Club*.

Fight Club was released a few months after we moved into our house, and something about the experience of watching it transformed Nick overnight. He went from being a weird nerd like the rest of us to an intolerable nightmare of a human

being. It wasn't just that Nick saw the movie and got excited
over it. It wasn't even that he walked away inspired by it. I legit-
imately think the experience of watching *Fight Club* rewired
the kid's brain chemistry. Afterward, he walked differently, his
posture self-assured and confident. He reacted to things differently, his love for Dungeons & Dragons replaced by an obsession with sports. The most evident change, however, was that
he talked differently. Inexplicably, he adopted an outdated hip-
hop vernacular and began referring to all of his roommates as
"Cousin."

"Yo, cousin, you want to get some food?" he asked no one in
particular as the assembled roommates hung out in our living
room one afternoon.

"Nah, Nick," Jesse said, "we all just ate. Sorry, man."

"Yo, cousin," Nick answered. "That's fine. Let's rock some
Tecmo Bowl, yo."

"Dude," Eric said, "stop calling everyone 'cousin.' And we're
not gonna play Tecmo Bowl right now, you can see that we're all
watching TV."

"Whattup, cousin?" Nick replied. "You busy being a studio
prankster?"

You have to realize that Nick was the most stiff, stuffy white
guy I'd ever met. His natural voice sounded like the one every
black stand-up comedian uses to mock white people. So to have
him call us "cousin" or a "mark ass buster," to have him throw fist
pounds and talk like a '90s rap-era gangsta, was at first amusing,
then confusing, and then, after a few days, deeply and pro-
foundly irritating.

After his *Fight Club*–driven renaissance, Nick somehow
managed to befriend a crew of guys from a nearby frat house.
He was thrilled to hang out with these guys, though it was clear

from the outside perspective that they brought him around as a joke. Nick once regaled us with a tale of how he'd gotten into a "fight" alongside his new buddies.

"You go out and get in fights now?" Mark asked.

"Yeah, cousin," Nick answered. "It's awesome. It's just like *Fight Club*. Fa' real."

"What happened?" Anthony asked.

"Well, we were at a party," Nick said. "And this guy stepped up. So I was like, 'Yo cousin what's the problem?'"

"Stop saying 'cousin,'" Eric interjected.

"So he kept talking shit, like a punk," Nick continued, "and my friends took him down. I ran up and kicked him a few times. It ruled."

"So you just kicked a guy who was already beaten up?" Jesse asked.

"Yeah, cousin," Nick answered. "No doubt."

"You understand that's not being in a fight, right?" Mark asked. "That's just kicking a guy when he's down."

"Word up," Nick answered.

No one believed Nick's stories and he must have sensed that his phony posturing was annoying all of us. It was obvious no one wanted to hang out with him, and he began to realize that when he was home people found excuses to leave. So in what was a deviously clever move, he tried to win back favor with our housemates by targeting me.

Meanwhile, I'd also spent the semester slowly losing my mind due to the physical condition of our house. It was completely disgusting. We'd all moved in thinking we would live that fun Animal House archetype, an anything-goes, lovable lifestyle. But in reality, living in filth and mayhem is unsanitary at best and maddening at worst. The smells that emanated from our kitchen didn't belong in first-world nations. I was the only roommate interested in cleaning and I once spent an hour searching our kitchen for the source of one foul stench, only to find a completely full gallon of milk under a pile of pizza boxes on the floor. Between the camel crickets and the stench, I was at my limit.

I begged my roommates to help me clean, and on a few occasions I lost it and yelled at them. Nick knew that the other roommates bristled at me for this. Nobody likes getting yelled at, especially when they're nineteen. Nick turned his insanity in my direction, and the other roommates egged him on, finding humor in how angry he could make me. If he couldn't get them to like him on his own he would try to bond with them by tormenting me.

I once came home to find Nick in my room, rifling through my mini-fridge. I'd wondered who'd been stealing my food for a while, and was glad to catch him in the act.

"Yo, cousin, you need to clean this thing out," Nick told me, nonplussed at being caught. "This pasta's been in here for, like, a week." He grinned and left. I became the butt of jokes about the incident for a full week or two.

On another occasion, I was alone in the living room watching television. Nick walked out of his bedroom and, for no reason, went up to the television and shut it off. Then he laughed at me and walked away.

"Yo, cousins," Nick said to the rest of the roommates later that night, right in front of me. "You should have seen it. I bitched Chris hard and he didn't do shit."

It was all beginning to add up, and the thing that finally pushed me over the edge was the infamous donut incident.

One night I came home from class and my roommates were sitting in our living room. I walked into the kitchen and saw a ravaged box of Dunkin' Donuts on our table. Icing was smeared everywhere and the torn and empty box lay on its side.

I calmly walked back to the living room.

"Guys, I don't know whose donuts these were, but they should probably clean up that mess before the camel crickets descend upon us," I said.

Some of my roommates snickered. Others looked awkward.

"Yeah," Nick grinned. "The owner of those donuts should clean them up."

Everybody laughed. I rolled my eyes and walked away. I wasn't going to play another one of Nick's weird games. The next day, Eric and I went out to lunch and he let me know that I had already been playing one unwittingly.

"Those were your donuts," he told me. "Your brother dropped by the house in the afternoon. Your mom sent the donuts with him. Nick ate all of them to fuck with you."

When I was in college, a dozen donuts were worth as much to me as roughly $4,000 cash would be today. I was heartbroken. My mom had sent them. And Forman had removed that act of goodwill from my life before I even knew about it. And eating twelve donuts in an hour isn't a pleasant experience. That can only be done as a malicious act. It's silly to say, but out of all the things Nick did to me, I don't think I would have hated him half as much if I'd been able to eat one measly donut.

It broke me. I spent as much time as possible outside of the house, and when I was home, I tended to sit in my room and avoid everyone. Nick had won.

~~~

That year I had joined a comedy troupe that performed shows one weekend a semester. Looking back on it now, I'd have to say the troupe wasn't at the cutting edge of comedy. We played those painful-to-watch improv games where you have to wear funny hats and shit, and where halfway through a scene you have to all of a sudden pretend you're Nicolas Cage, things like that. But it was my introduction to performing, the first comedy I'd done, and it was the only thing I cared about. I wanted it to go well. I needed to prove that I had what it took, and if I bombed I wouldn't be asked back.

As that semester's shows approached I told a few of my friends about it, and word spread to my roommates. Of course, Nick heard about it, too, and despite the fact that he and I never spoke anymore, he tagged along. The show was going along fine until about five minutes before intermission.

"Yo," a voice shouted from the crowd. I froze as I recognized it was Nick.

"That girl," he continued, "is not funny."

The crowd gasped, and my friend Jill, who was in the middle of a scene, went white with embarrassment. A dark energy came over the room as Nick continued to heckle us intermittently.

After intermission, he launched into a full-on assault.

Among the many things he shouted were the phrases "Chris Gethard is a trick ass bitch," "Fuck you studio pranksters," and the one that he repeated over thirty times for no reason, "Free Mumia." He was relentless.

Afterward, I was furious. The show had been ruined and since Nick was there because of me, I was responsible. The cast told me not to worry about it. We hung out that night and I didn't get home until late. The next morning, I wrapped a towel around my waist and headed upstairs to take a shower.

To my surprise, a dozen of my friends and roommates were gathered in our living room. Sitting in the middle, holding court, was Nick. When I entered, everyone stopped talking. I continued toward the bathroom. I had no interest in reinitiating the drama from the previous night, but Nick had other plans.

"Yo, cousin," he said, "you want to talk about what happened?"

"Nah, I'm good," I replied, "let's just forget about it." I smiled and kept going.

"I had one thing I wanted to say," he yelled from behind me. I stopped.

"At least one of us was funny last night."

Everyone burst out laughing. I had officially reached my breaking point. Steal my food? Sure. Target me for the amusement of others? Why not? Insult my friends? You're pushing it, but if they manage to calm me down we'll be fine. Tell me I'm not funny? Apparently that's what it took to send me into an unrestrained blackout rage. I turned and sprinted into the room, holding my towel tightly around my waist.

"What the fuck is your problem, dude?" I screamed in Nick's face. "What are you going for? You want to fucking fight me? Let's fucking fight, then."

Dumbfounded, Nick just stared at me. The room was completely silent.

"It's been all year with this fucking bullshit," I shouted. "Why don't you fucking get up and fight me right now, motherfucker?"

There was a long pause. Nick was frozen with confusion, and the rest of the onlookers were horrified—either at my behavior or at the sight of my pale, spindly body. There was a long stretch of quiet as Nick stared at me. Finally, he realized I wasn't going to back down this time.

"Are you crazy?" he said, laughing. "I'm so much bigger than you. I'll kill you."

"I don't fucking think so, man," I shouted. "But fine, get up and fucking beat the shit out of me. That way we can all fucking move on."

Nick sat still. He was no longer laughing. He looked scared. Scared of a pasty guy he outweighed by forty pounds, who was wearing nothing but a towel.

"Come on," I said. "Let's fucking do it. Let's fucking fight, you pussy. Stand up."

He remained frozen. He couldn't look anyone in the eye. He stared at the floor.

"You fucking pussy, *stand up*," I screamed. "Are you just gonna sit there?"

Nick started to speak, then stopped. He cleared his throat.

"What, motherfucker?" I asked.

"Fine," he said, his voice shaking. "Let me just put my contacts in."

He sat still, staring at me.

"Did you just say . . . put your contacts in?" Jesse asked, shaking his head.

Eric started laughing.

"Dude . . . ," he said, "you're a fucking pussy."

"Put your contacts in?" our friend Sean echoed.

The room erupted in laughter. Nick had postured for a full year; then, when the moment of truth came, he buckled.

I, on the other hand, had shown I was willing to drop my towel and fight him, nude, in front of a dozen people. After a year of being Nick's whipping boy, I needed only five short minutes of crazy behavior to earn back the respect of my friends.

Nick finally got up and went into his room.

For a few minutes, we waited uncomfortably in the living room for him to reemerge, contacts applied, so that he and I could fight.

He never came back out.

There was a fresh round of comments regarding what a pussy Nick was, and a handful of apologies thrown in my direction.

Then I took a shower. I washed off not just the funk of the party the night before but a year's worth of being pushed around and insulted.

I saw Nick only three or four times after we stopped living together. Largely, we ignored each other. There wasn't any real closure. The closest we came was one night at a bar, years after we'd graduated, when he approached me.

"Yo," he said. "I've always wanted to tell you something."

"What's that?" I asked.

"I was a dick because I was jealous," he said. "I always wanted to do comedy."

The mutual misery of our situation hit me in the gut. It never even occurred to me that he might be jealous of me, because I was such a depressed person I never would have seen any aspect of my life as being worthy of jealousy. But I was pursuing comedy; he was a funny guy who never did anything with it. He desperately wanted to fight but didn't quite have it in him; I was begrudgingly willing to do so. It dawned on me that we were very similar people. Only I was proactive and he wasn't. I went through with things and he didn't. And it must have driven him crazy.

Since Nick left my life, I've become better about forgiving people who do bad things to me. Because I learned long ago from a former friend that you don't really have enemies; you only have people who are somehow more miserable than you are.

The World's Foremost Goat

"You stop it!" I shouted. "You stop it right now!"

I braced myself. Koko, the alpha female of the barn, again lowered her head and charged straight into my hip. She wasn't listening to my pleading commands. Signing up for joke classes wasn't turning out to be as funny as I thought it'd be.

A lot of college seniors will take an easy joke class to help them cruise by during their last semester. For its part, Rutgers was happy to oblige them with a course catalogue that offered a number of highly coveted options. Wine Tasting always filled up instantly. Acting 101 was a go-to because it was open to the general student body and amazingly easy; real actors went to the Mason Gross School of the Arts, a sub-school of Rutgers. Most infamous was Theater Appreciation, an English department offering where you simply saw a bunch of Broadway shows.

Of course, I'm me and I always have to be one baby step crazier than anyone else I know. So every time one of my friends bragged about how he'd just found an easy course, I took it as a challenge to find one even more ludicrous. I spent hours scouring the Rutgers course listings until I found a course so weird that I knew I'd come out on top.

This is how I came to register for Animal Grooming, Husbandry, and Exhibition. Section: Goat.

Rutgers is split into a number of campuses. The College Avenue campus is what people think of when they think of a college. Douglass Campus is female housing only. Busch Campus is an engineering school, so it's only for Asians. Mason Gross is where you go if you like both smoking pot and overachieving. Livingston Campus is where they stick the weirdos, like people with misdemeanor convictions or Asperger's.

Cook Campus is the most mysterious of all. It's dedicated to the study of agriculture. The only people I ever met who attended Cook were exercise science majors. They were like the emissaries from a strange land who occasionally visited the normal world, but otherwise stuck to their own. Most of the Cook kids hung out in weird barns set far back in fields. Rumors swirled of a "cow with a window in its stomach" that lived there. For all the normal people who didn't attend Cook, there was no reason to go there.

That's why most Rutgers students didn't know there was a class on goats.

For the class, I had to wake up extremely early. I didn't like that at all. I had to take a bus to the end of its line. I didn't like that either. I had to hang out in a barn. Also not my thing.

But I got to do something incredibly weird, and that made it all worthwhile.

Before my first class, before I even saw my goat, I decided to name it "Jeffrey Timmons, World's Foremost Goat." I don't know why. I don't know anyone named Timmons, and have no particular affinity for the name Jeffrey. It just felt right at the time.

Entering the barn for the first time, I was instantly over-whelmed. I'd never set foot on a real farm in my life, and there were a lot of things I wasn't expecting. For example, I always thought pigs made a sound that goes something like "oink oink." What I found was that pigs actually make a sound that resembles a woman being brutally murdered. They weren't even in the same building as I was; I could hear them screaming from the next barn over.

Inside the barn where my class was held, the goats charged chaotically around a large pen. There were roughly twenty of them, along with their kids. I arrived with no idea of what I was supposed to do, so I approached a young woman who was hurl-ing piles of hay into the goat pen while the goats ran in circles and shrieked.

"I think I'm taking a class here," I screamed over the goat screeches.

"Oh, right," she sighed. She stopped hurling hay. "Here's how it works. You walk around with your goat. Get to know your goat. Feed the goat from your hand. Keep your goat clean. Then at the end of the semester, you'll compete in the goat show."

"The goat show?" I asked.

"Yes, the goat show," she said. "Each year Cook holds Ag Field Day. The goat show takes place there."

"Ag Field?" I asked.

"Yeah, Ag Field Day," she said, getting frustrated. "The agri-cultural celebration Cook holds every year."

She apparently didn't know that to me, the customs of Cook Campus were as foreign and mysterious as the customs of gyp-sies or Freemasons. Fearing I would irritate her more, I backed off my line of questioning.

"That goat's yours," she said.

She pointed to a tan-colored goat eating by herself in the corner. While most of the goats were social and jockeying for position, my goat seemed shy and removed. Two tiny goats played underneath her.

"Those are her kids, 5226 and 5227," the girl said. "Your goat's name is Sugar."

"No, it's not," I said. "My goat's name is Jeffrey Timmons, World's Foremost Goat. I already named him."

"Her," the girl said. "No male goats. If we brought a male goat in here, it would just try to fuck everyone."

Her reasoning was sound, but her attitude made it clear that she couldn't care less about my presence in her barn.

"Well, I'm sticking with my name anyway," I said.

I wasn't sure if she was my teacher, so I stood around waiting for her to approve or disapprove of my clinging to the name I'd arbitrarily given my goat. She was far more interested in the affairs of the goats she was feeding than she was in the ways of men. She didn't even turn back toward me before mumbling the words "I don't care."

I walked toward Jeffrey Timmons, World's Foremost Goat. She backed away, looking at me suspiciously. She neighed at me, but weakly. She was tired.

I'm not completely sure why, but for some reason I immediately identified with this goat. I don't know if I've ever fallen harder for an animal on first sight. I've never been a pet guy. I didn't grow up with dogs and have honestly never understood the appeal. From visiting friends with dogs, it seemed to me that their main effect on the lives of their owners is that they disrupt meals and also you have to pick up their shit with your hands. My family had cats when I was growing up, which I liked better because at least cats know how to do their own thing and stay out of your way.

Yet somehow, the girl running the barn had managed to ally me with a goat version of me. This goat seemed worn out, tired, and confused. I empathized deeply. I looked into her creepy goat eyes and what I saw was a kindred spirit looking back at me.

At that moment another goat sprinted across the barn and slammed as hard as she could into the side of my goat.

This was Koko.

Here's my opinion of Koko to this day: fuck Koko. She was the alpha female of the barn. Some of the other goats actually tried to stand up to her as she went out of her way to jump and spit on them. Others ran away or, even worse, just took it. I was flabbergasted. The world of goats, I found out, revolves completely around bullying. The worst bully gets her food first, gets pampered the most, and disrupts any situation that doesn't directly benefit her.

Immediately, I despised Koko. After all, I was the human version of Jeffrey Timmons, and I'd known far too many human versions of Koko.

In order to get credit for the class I was required to put in three hours a week with Jeffrey Timmons. There were no set times for this, so I could show up any time the barn was open. Some days, I'd be the only person in the yard practicing with my goat. Practicing entailed walking around in circles, training Jeffrey to stay by my side at all times. I was told that there were three primary ways to make this happen: give Jeffrey Timmons treats, pet Jeffrey Timmons, and talk to Jeffrey Timmons.

Petting a goat is weird, but you get used to it fast. They don't react with happiness like dogs or cats do. Mostly, they just stand still and stare off into the distance. Really, the only aspect of petting Jeffrey Timmons that I never got completely used to was seeing her shit. When goats shit they basically stop midstride and eject hundreds of little shit pebbles onto the ground. So while petting Jeffrey Timmons was all good, I quickly found that petting Jeffrey Timmons while her ass spit weird droplets of shit everywhere was disconcerting.

Feeding Jeffrey turned out to be a breeze. Especially since I cheated. I was supposed to feed Jeffrey feed from the barn. But in my first few days with Jeffrey Timmons, I noticed that goats get distracted really fast. Even with feed, I couldn't hold her attention span for as long as I needed to. So one day, as a potential solution, I brought in a pocketful of Cap'n Crunch cereal. That changed everything. As soon as she got a taste of it, she was obsessed with me. I'd show up at the barn and she'd immediately focus in and make a beeline toward me. Not even Koko's ramming could halt her in her tracks. I had randomly discovered that Cap'n Crunch is essentially goat crack. It did wonders for our bonding.

While I managed to get petting and feeding down pat, the only bonding exercise that did get weird was talking to Jeffrey Timmons. When we were in the yard alone together, I noticed a strange pattern developing. Away from the chaos of the barn, the aggressiveness of Koko, the constant neediness of 5226 and 5227, Jeffrey would immediately relax. She wouldn't neigh as much, she was less twitchy, and she'd move at a more relaxed pace.

"I know, Jeffrey Timmons, World's Foremost Goat," I once found myself saying. "It's nice to get away from all that stuff for a little while. Believe me, I know that things can get hard. I sometimes feel like I'm in over my head, too."

This was a period of my life when I didn't talk to anyone about my problems. I routinely told my mother I was using my school's mental health services to get therapy. I wasn't. I regularly told my ex-girlfriend that I was going to start seeing someone. I never did. It wasn't just that I wasn't getting help, I was lying to people I cared about in order to avoid it. Not only could I not talk to those people about my problems, I couldn't even talk to them about maybe finding other people who I *could* talk to about my problems. And yet, here I found myself able to open up to a goat. And as the semester went on, this habit snowballed.

"This girl really liked me, Jeffrey, and I didn't kiss her," I told my goat. "*She* asked *me* out. And she was awesome. Beautiful, smart, nice. And the date went great. You know why I didn't do it?"

Jeffrey stared at me as she devoured a low-hanging branch of evergreen tree.

"I like her too much to stick her with me," I continued. "I'm such a fucking mess that I didn't want to ruin her with my fucking bullshit."

Jeffrey looked me in the eye as she continued chewing. Then promptly shit a tidal wave of pebbles all over the ground.

As the semester passed by and the day of our competition grew close, I began getting nervous. Most of the other participants were agriculture majors who actually knew what they were doing (because why would you take a class on goat grooming, husbandry, and exhibition if you weren't in that field?). I, meanwhile, was clueless as to what the competition even entailed.

The only chance I stood lay in the fact that Jeffrey Timmons was a former show goat. A lot of the goats in the barn were born and raised there, but a handful were old pros from the competitive goat circuit who had been donated by their owners when they aged past their prime. Jeffrey was one of these rare goats. She was used to being put through the motions of goat competition. I just had to trust that her instincts remained intact and that when the moment of truth came she would step up to the plate.

Late in the afternoon the day before our competition, I visited Jeffrey Timmons one last time at the barn.

"I've told you a lot of stuff this semester," I said to her out loud. "You've really been there for me. You're a good friend. Tomorrow, do your best. Even if we come in last place, I'll still be your friend."

Jeffrey ate Cap'n Crunch out of my hand. She didn't react to my speech. I assume she was playing it cool because even she found it humiliating that I was pouring my heart out to a goat.

When I let her back into the pen she headed straight for 5226 and 5227, but before she could get to them, Koko sprinted from the far corner and slammed head-first into Jeffrey Timmons's side. Jeffrey let out a yelp of pain.

"Hey!" I yelled. "Stop!"

Without thinking, I leapt forward, landing in front of Koko just as she crouched low and got ready to ram Jeffrey Timmons again.

"You stop it!" I shouted. "You stop it right now!"

I backed into the corner of the barn as she huffed and prepared to charge at me. She wasn't listening. She charged full force and rammed into my hip at full speed.

"Koko!" I bellowed. "You stop!"

She snorted and ran at me again. She hit me, and I reached down and grabbed her by the head. She bucked wildly, trying to get away from me.

"Stop with your nonsense," I said, maintaining my grip. "Stop being mean, you asshole bully."

She tore loose from my hands and glared angrily at me. I stared back at her. Finally, she turned and trotted away. I turned back and saw Jeffrey Timmons standing meekly against the wall, her two children wrestling with each other below her.

"You're welcome," I said. It was the least I could do.

With that I climbed over the wall of the pen. As I left the barn, the girl in charge gave me the exact look that the type of weirdo who fights goats and also talks to them deserves.

The next morning, I woke up at six and headed back to Cook. I had to prepare Jeffrey Timmons, World's Foremost Goat, for our big competition. This involved a three-step process that I had been dreading: I had to shave her, clip her toenails, and shampoo her.

On my way to the bus stop, I stopped in the convenience store where I bought my Cap'n Crunch for Jeffrey. To my dismay they were all out. *This is a bad way to start competition day,* I thought. It was then that I realized that at some point, in spite of everything, I'd actually come to take this competition very, very seriously. I know that all athletes have routines. Jeffrey's involved consuming Cap'n Crunch from my hand. This hiccup in our regular preparation was not good on competition day. I prayed that she wasn't too discerning a cereal addict as I grabbed a box of Honeycomb instead and ran to catch the bus.

Jeffrey Timmons was okay with being shaved. She didn't like the sound of the electric clippers, but did seem to enjoy not being covered in thick hair. However, she did not like having her toenails clipped, and I didn't enjoy doing it either. Clipping a goat's toenails involves placing the goat on a wooden stand and having four agriculture majors hold her still while you take what looks like a pair of pliers and cut her toenails in half, or until they start bleeding. In my case it also involved having one of those agriculture majors quickly sense my vast incompetence before taking over and doing it for me.

Unfortunately, Jeffrey Timmons liked being shampooed even less than the toenail clipping. I took her outside to an asphalt patch behind the barn, where I tied her to a fence. I sprayed her with icy cold water from a hose, and she hated me for it. She hissed, cried, and tried to run away. I rubbed shampoo all over her body and hosed her down again. When we were done, she was visibly upset with me. Any goodwill I'd earned from fending off Koko was out the window.

I tried to calm her down by feeding her Honeycomb, but it didn't work. It turns out that goats hate Honeycomb. To my palate it's pretty close to Cap'n Crunch, but Jeffrey Timmons disagreed. After eating just a few, she actually refused them. I was amazed. After all, goats will eat license plates if you don't stop them. I guess it doesn't say much for Honeycomb.

Jeffrey was clearly off her game, and I was freaking out. We were moments away from entering the circle for the competition. The other goatherds stood with their goats calmly by their sides; Jeffrey paced back and forth angrily and refused to come to me when I called for her.

I didn't know what to do and went into a near-catatonic panic. I stared straight ahead, and when one of the girls at the barn told me to get ready, I couldn't even answer. Luckily, my stare locked onto a solution I hadn't even thought of.

I quickly ran down the hill to the fir tree Jeffrey liked chewing on. She had stripped all the lower branches, but luckily, I am taller than a goat. I tore off a few branches and ran back to her. She devoured them, and miraculously, it calmed her down.

"You ready?" I asked her. I petted her, squatted down, and looked her in the eye.

When I walked back toward the other competitors, she dutifully followed and stood by my side.

Then we entered the circle—a low fence surrounded by spectators—and did a lap with the other competing pairs. We stood in our spot until the judge instructed us to walk across the pen and back. I had no idea how this was supposed to work, but

Jeffrey did. When we got to the end of the pen, I awkwardly turned, but she stood still and looked at me. I realized that I was turning clockwise, toward her, and if I did, we'd bump into each other. Jeffrey waited for me to realize my mistake. I paused and turned counterclockwise, and she turned away from me. We completed our circle and triumphantly walked back together.

The other competitors took their turns. The judge walked around the circle, sizing up all of the competitors. He walked to one pair and handed them the blue ribbon. The crowd politely applauded.

Then, he walked up to Koko and spoke with her handler. Unfortunately, they were a few spots in front of me, so I couldn't hear their conversation.

Please, not Koko, I thought to myself. *Any other goat, but I don't want Jeffrey Timmons to get beat by Koko. I don't want to get beat by Koko.*

The judge smiled at Koko's handler. Then, he turned and walked toward me.

"How have you liked your semester?" he asked me. I was stunned to be in the running.

"It's been great," I said. "I've really bonded with my goat, Jeffrey Timmons, the World's Foremost Goat."

"You know she's a girl, right?" he asked.

"Yes, sir," I answered. "I named her before I knew we only worked with females."

He smiled and asked, "What's the most surprising quality of Jeffrey Timmons you've discovered in your time at the barn?"

I thought long and hard. Then, I lied.

"Her relationship with her children, 5226 and 5227," I answered. "I assumed before I started that goats didn't have much personality. She's very affectionate with them, which I didn't expect. There's real emotion in these goats."

He nodded, impressed. While on some level I did believe in what I said, I knew he would have thought I was a complete maniac if I had given him my real answer—*"She's a really good listener."*

The judge then stepped back to the middle of the circle. He looked toward Koko. Then he turned and looked at Jeffrey Timmons, the World's Foremost Goat.

Finally, he stepped toward us, and he handed me the red ribbon.

We had placed second in a low-stakes competitive goat show I signed up for as a joke. I stood and smiled at the judge. Just under the surface, I was freaking out. It's fair to say that winning this goat show was the greatest athletic achievement of my life. Externally, I was some idiot standing next to a goat way too early on a weekend morning. Internally, I knew what Aaron Boone felt like when he hit that home run against the Red Sox. I knew what Larry Johnson felt like when he hit that four-point play in the play-offs. I understood the thrill of achieving great heights, even though my great heights sadly involved standing in a small wire circle in the middle of a field while fifteen to twenty apathetic weirdos stood around fairly wondering why a goat show would even take place on a college campus.

After our red ribbon performance Jeffrey and I went on to the winner's circle. Here, the two best goats from each preliminary round faced off. The competition was fierce; some of the seniors from Cook had been working with their goats for all four years. This time, Jeffrey and I didn't place.

It didn't matter to me at all. We'd won. Because even while we had our asses handed to us in the winner's circle, I still had the privilege of looking out over the fence at Koko, who was now running around the field behind us head-butting the other loser goats.

"We're the worst of the winners," I said quietly to Jeffrey Timmons. She gently bumped into the side of my leg as the judge walked by. She looked up at me. I can't be sure, but I think she felt the same quiet pride I did.

Then, she shit everywhere.

My Lows at Loews

If you hate yourself with a passion but are too much of a coward to commit suicide, I highly suggest you apply for a job at the Loews Cineplex on Route 1 in New Brunswick, New Jersey.

I was hired to work there the summer after my freshman year of college, and I immediately realized two things that spelled doom for my prospects of survival. The first was that the employees there had a built-in social scene. They hung out after work, acted chummy on the job, and made it clear who the cool kids were. The second was that I didn't have a chance of being included in that scene at all.

"Hey, Lynne, you doing anything tonight?" I was pouring butter into a dispenser when I overheard James, one of my assistant managers, inviting Lynne, a blonde sex addict who was filling popcorn bins, out for the evening.

"Nah," she replied. "Are people doing something?"

"Yeah," he said. "There's a house party at Ray's place. Probably starting up at like ten or eleven. You should definitely come."

"I'll go," Lynne said. "That sounds like fun."

"Cool," James said. He turned toward the area where I was working.

"Erik," James called out, "you should come too. And Marcus, definitely swing by if you're down."

Erik was on one side of me, Marcus on the other. No one even pretended it was uncomfortable to ignore my existence. It was a caste system, where every other person I worked with was in one caste and I was the lone member of some reviled lowly tribe.

Sadly, this experience was not completely unfamiliar to me. I would say that about 80 percent of the time, people's first impression of me is something along the lines of "Oh, I get this guy. He's nice and funny and completely nonthreatening. I like him." Unfortunately, the other 20 percent of the time, the reaction I inspire is one of hatred and a desire for annihilation. No mercy, no remorse.

At Loews, nearly the entire staff reacted in the latter fashion.

To be fair, two people did talk to me. One was a kid named Ayale who spoke to everyone, because he was a born-again Christian and was constantly trying to convert anyone willing to hear him out. In normal life, a conversion-hungry born-again is someone I would have avoided at all costs. But my sense of isolation was such that Ayale became a confidante. I even started offering him rides home after I found out he usually walked miles to his apartment in Highland Park each night after our shift.

"Ayale, you want a ride?" I shouted out my car window one night as he began his trudge up Route 1. It was late, after 2:30 A.M. We'd been held after that night as punishment because someone had poured excess butter into the drain of the soda machine rather than placing it back in the bottle to be reused the next day. That person was me. In my view it had been an act of protest against the cinema's policy of reusing melted butter day after day. For my coworkers it was simply another reason to hate me even more.

"Sure, man," Ayale said, jumping into the car. "You a good man, Chris. You a good man. Jesus would like you."

"Oh, uh, thanks," I replied. "I can't believe they kept us so late tonight."

"Yeah, they be working us hard," he answered, his creepy, unceasing Christian grin directed toward me. "But hard work is good now, man, because in the next life it definitely gonna pay off."

"Oh. . . . Right," I said, turning onto his block. "Well, I guess I'll see you tomorrow, dude. I'll be the one no one's talking to."

Instead of getting out of the car, Ayale stared deeply into my eyes. If he wasn't a born-again, I would have thought he was coming on to me. Although, in the context of his world, I guess he was.

"Chris, man, you funny. You really funny. We should hang out," he said. Then, he did his best to sound nonchalant. "You should REALLY come to church with me."

I pretended not to hear him, lightly nodding along to the music in my car as he maintained eye contact.

"You should REALLY come to church," he continued. After another pause, he reiterated it with a simple but forceful "REALLY."

Again, I simply chose not to react, and instead maintained the body language and facial expression of someone who hadn't heard the same invitation three times in a row. Eventually, Ayale got the message and sauntered out of the car, thanking me multiple times for my charity in giving him a ride.

That exact exchange happened between Ayale and me at least seven times during my summer working at Loews.

The only other guy who talked to me at work was Rhoderick, an immigrant from Ghana who was the nicest man I'd ever met. He was simply so happy to be there, working. He would cover anyone's shift, giving it his all, a smile always emerging from behind his bushy, graying beard. Whatever atrocities he may have faced in his home country, this pit of hell that was the Loews Cineplex was obviously heaven in comparison.

One day I had to work the early shift, and when I showed up at the theater, the doors were still locked. The only other person there waiting for management was Rhoderick. He was sitting on the curb in front of the main entrance, whistling to himself.

"Jeez, Rhoderick," I said as I approached him. "I thought *I* was here early."

"Man, I been here for an hour," he said, smiling. "I like to get up early, yeah? Just walk around, breathe the air. Listen to the birds. The sunlight . . . it's beautiful."

"Yeah, dude," I said, pausing a moment to look around. "Yeah. I guess the sunlight is beautiful."

"In my country," he said, "it was hard to remember the sun."

As with many things Rhoderick said, I chose to allow it to sit unexplained, knowing that any elaboration would replace the vague semi-hilarity of his statement with the brutal realities of whatever that statement meant.

Ayale and Rhoderick were outsiders in their own respective ways, the only people close to my lowly depths in the society of Loews Cineplex. Aside from my occasional conversation with them, my shifts at Loews were spent in almost complete social isolation. I certainly didn't win myself any points with the staff or my manager the night I nearly got myself fired and the theater sued. Late one Saturday, a friend and I went to see the Omar Epps/Taye Diggs vehicle *The Wood*. Neither of us had any particular interest in seeing the movie, but since we were poor and since I got two free tickets through work, we went. The theater was completely sold out, filled mostly with people from Staten Island who came over the bridge because our theater had an awesome sound system.

About halfway through the movie, there was a ruckus. I turned to see two women yelling at each other about halfway up the stadium seating.

"Bitch, mind your business," one woman shouted, "before you get yolked up!"

The other woman lunged at her. Her man was barely able to hold her back.

"Bitch," she shouted. "Don't be telling me what the fuck I can and cannot do."

The first girl responded by picking up her extra-large-sized soda and throwing it into the second girl's face. The women simultaneously broke free from the men who had been attempting to hold them back and went at each other. Rather than trying to reestablish control, both men reacted by brutally fist-fighting each other right there in the seats. The position they were standing in was perfect for projecting the silhouettes of the tops of their heads onto the screen, providing all in attendance the rare pleasure of watching hair-pulling, punch-throwing shadows share the screen with the charming and talented Mr. Taye Diggs.

One of the men bellowed, "Bitch, that's why you're wearing my soda," and the entire theater erupted in applause for the insult. The roar of the crowd only fueled the fighting spirit of the two couples, and eventually they tumbled down the aisle and out the emergency exit beneath the screen.

At that point, I went back to watching the movie.

On Monday my manager approached me, baffled.

"Chris," he said, "is it true you were in that theater the other night when a fight broke out?"

"Yeah . . . ," I answered, not sure what he was getting at. It was rare for a manager to talk to a lowly floor worker. Usually that was left to the assistant managers. Besides, I was busy trying to restack Goobers during another shiftlong stint of being treated like a leper.

"Why didn't you do anything?" he asked, raising his arms up in disbelief.

"I wasn't working that night," I said. "I was just there watching."

"But you couldn't do anything?" he asked, truly unable to fathom my reaction. "You couldn't even come get someone who was working?"

I shrugged my shoulders. "I guess I didn't think of it."

"Chris," he said, shaking his head with genuine sadness in his eyes. "They went out in the parking lot and fought with knives."

The sad truth of the matter is that I neglected stopping a knife fight mostly because I was happy to get back to watching the movie. This was in spite of the fact that I wasn't too into the movie. It was the principle of the thing. I'd like to think that I'm the type of guy who steps up to the plate and intervenes in such situations. But I also know that I spend a majority of my time in my own world, and when I was nineteen years old it never would have occurred to me that preventing a fistfight is just a good thing to do whether you're on the clock or not. Still, that incident qualifies as only the third-lowest moment that happened to me during my tenure at Loews.

For all the downsides, the one perk of working at Loews was the gracious opportunity to see movies for free. During the summer of 1999 that single perk nearly made up for everything. Because when it came to movies, that summer was a nerd's dream. It was the summer *The Sixth Sense, The Blair Witch Project*, and a number of other hot movies came out. But above all else, it was the summer of *Star Wars: Episode I—The Phantom Menace.*

I was nineteen, so I wasn't old enough to go to bars. I had no money and very few friends. Seeing movies for free was a saving grace that gave me something to do at night.

That was how I wound up seeing *The Phantom Menace* thirteen times in the theater.

My entire summer was spent watching that deplorable relaunch of the Star Wars franchise over and over again. I stopped after viewing thirteen only because my behavior that day has led to emotional scars that cut deeper than most people's hatred of Jar Jar Binks.

At some point during the movie, I realized that I was hungry. Unfortunately, while the theater offered free tickets to employees, it did not offer food or drink. Considering that I was broke, I was shit out of luck. By this point *The Phantom Menace* had been out for a few weeks, and word had spread that it was unwatchable. I was there for an afternoon showing, and was entirely alone.

As I sat in the theater, my hunger continued to grow and my mind began to wander. I knew who was on duty, and realized there was a good chance the theater hadn't been cleaned all day. I scoured the aisles until I found a half-full bag of popcorn, which then, without much hesitation, I ate. In other words, I put someone else's garbage into my mouth. Their grubby, greasy fingers had likely picked up and dropped a large percentage of the popcorn I was now eating. It probably would have been healthier to place the unwashed fingers of a homeless man directly into my mouth.

But for some reason, not only did I eat a bag of filthy garbage I picked up off a Cineplex floor, I didn't even feel bad about it. My summer had gone so terribly and I had been pushed to such a point of social isolation that my descent into becoming a scavenger for another human being's trash didn't even depress me at the time. Not even while watching *The Phantom Menace*. This job had pushed me as close to subhuman as I have ever been.

Sadly, the slope was a slippery one and the popcorn had made me thirsty. I went to the garbage can and picked out an old cup. I went to the soda fountain and discretely refilled it when none of my coworkers were watching. I placed my lips onto the rim of the cardboard cup, where a stranger's teeth marks still remained, and washed it all down with Cherry Coke.

And yet, eating and drinking garbage while watching *The Phantom Menace* for the thirteenth time wasn't even my lowest point that summer.

That sad day came when I rebelled against the internal politics of Loews Cineplex in an ill-conceived act of defiance that came back to haunt me in multiple ways.

Have you ever wondered what happens to all those cool-ass posters, banners, and cardboard cutouts you see in movie theaters? At Loews, there was a particularly spiteful assistant manager named Bassie whose job it was to dole them out as prizes for the employees. He would choose, based purely on his will and his personal feelings, who would get what. That summer, between *Star Wars*, *Eyes Wide Shut*, and *The Blair Witch Project*, there were a lot of cool, valuable promotional items the staff was jockeying to get their hands on.

I received exactly two posters. One was for a Claire Danes movie called *Brokedown Palace*, where Ms. Danes gets locked in a Thai prison. I gave the poster to my Thai friend Jan. The other was for a Ted Danson vehicle called *Mumford*, which, to this day, I'm not even sure was ever released.

The poster distribution was the most definitive way in which status was shown at the theater. The higher-ups certified whom they accepted as part of the in-crowd by giving them cool stuff. I got the message. I was the Mumford of the staff.

One day, after a particularly miserable daytime shift, Bassie and a few of his cronies were behind the service desk. I walked by on my way out, staring at the floor.

"Hey, Chris," Bassie said with a sneer. "Want that?" The employees standing with him snickered, and a cocky grin inched across his face.

Bassie pointed across the lobby to a stand-up cardboard contraption promoting *Inspector Gadget* starring Matthew Broderick. It was a 3-D display and had all sorts of gears and gizmos popping out at different depths, all anchored to a heavy cardboard base.

Everyone chuckled and something inside me clicked. I'd officially had enough. Instead of shrugging off his offer, which was only meant to make fun of me, I looked him dead in the eye.

"Sure," I said. "I'll take it."

They all looked confused. The display was about twelve feet high and three feet thick. There was no way it was going to fit into a car, and no clear way to take it apart without destroying it.

Still, something inside my brain had snapped back into place and my pride returned, if only for a brief moment. I remembered what my life was like before I was eating garbage. I got mad that I wasn't being invited to parties with Lynne the sex addict. I became furious that my only friend was a Christian hellbent on converting me to a cultlike sect of born-agains. All of the emotions I had managed to turn off in order to work at this demeaning job came flooding back all at once, overwhelming me. I hated that I'd taken so much shit for so long. And here I was, being laughed at by the very authorities who had created and fostered this environment. I figured it was time to call their bluff.

I walked across the theater, grabbed the display, tipped it onto its side, and dragged it out the door. As I walked past the desk where Bassie and the others sat, straining to pull the heavy cube behind me, they all seemed confused. I took this as a sign of victory. I had beaten them by baffling them.

When I got to my car, I quickly confirmed that there was no way to fit the behemoth into my back seat. Nonetheless, I had proven my point. I wasn't going to let the powers that be at the Loews Cineplex laugh at me ever again. Instead, I would destroy them by making them think I was weird, if not borderline crazy. Mission accomplished. If nothing else, I was certain that now they would at least leave me the fuck alone.

I decided to drag the cutout to the dumpster out back and call it a day. But when I got there, Rhoderick was throwing cardboard into the thresher.

"Hey, man!" he said, with a level of joy that can be attained only by a man who has escaped his Hutu tormentors. "What are you doing?"

"I'm just gonna throw this thing out, Rhoderick," I said, sheepishly.

"What?" He seemed so sad. "But it's beautiful!"

"I really don't—" I began, but he cut me off before I could finish my sentence.

"You MUST keep it!"

His voice was deep with conviction. His eyes locked into mine, and the burning intensity within them let me know that the ability to own a twelve-foot-tall *Inspector Gadget* promotional cutout defined to this man everything beautiful about America.

"Okay," I said. There was nothing else to say. I had taken the display because I was willing to look crazy as long as it pissed off the management at a shitty multiplex on the side of a New Jersey highway. But I wasn't willing to look wasteful and un- grateful in front of someone who had been through so much. I was being defiant, fighting back against the powers that be, but Rhoderick was an instant reminder that my reality remained a very privileged one despite any issues I had. I was willing to look crazy to piss off and confuse the snobs I worked with. I wasn't willing to follow through so hard that I broke the heart of a man who I assumed had been through enough already.

Rhoderick told me to drag the cutout back to my car. He would find some rope. He seemed not just enthusiastic but driven. He took off running and met me at my car a few minutes later, holding piles of shredded clear plastic in his hand.

"I couldn't find any rope," he said, grinning, "so I made some!" Rhoderick had torn apart a handful of clear garbage bags and braided them together. The effort he put in only further re- iterated to me that I had made my bed and now I had to lie in it. He hoisted the cardboard cutout onto the top of my car and told me to get inside. While he passed his homemade rope through the windows and lashed it above the cutout I sat in the car, listening to him grunt as he strained to tighten the knots. After a few minutes, I heard him muttering in satisfaction. Cov- ered in sweat, he walked to the window and tenderly put his hand on my shoulder.

"Go home," he said, "and enjoy this."

His eyes wandered off toward the Raritan River, where the set- ting sun was reflecting off of the muddy brown water. Rhoderick smiled, and a soft chuckle escaped his lips. His mind was clearly elsewhere.

I hit the gas and drove about ten feet before the wind caught underneath the cutout, lifting it up against the "rope" and slamming it down onto the roof with a thud. I screeched to a halt.

"Rhoderick," I said, leaning out the window. "This isn't a good idea. I'm just gonna throw it away."

"No!" he scolded me. "It is yours. You *must* take it home. If it starts to fly off, just reach up and grab it with your hand. You will be fine."

"Yeah," I said. "That sounds good."

I sat in the car, hoping Rhoderick would make his way inside so I could drive over to the dumpster and throw out both the cutout and the piles of plastic tied to my car. Instead, he stood with his hands on his hips and grinned at me. After a few very awkward moments, I was left with no choice but to drive home, using two major highways, with a giant *Inspector Gadget* display strapped to the top of my 1986 Chevy Celebrity.

I made my way out onto Route 1, and had to go only 150 yards before merging onto Route 18. But in this short span, the cutout caught the wind and began bouncing off the top of my car. Taking Rhoderick's advice, I reached up and grabbed at it with my left hand. It lifted me off my seat. If I hadn't been wearing my seat belt, I would have been sucked out of the window and tossed onto the busy highway.

Panicking, I threw my hazard lights on and merged onto Route 18. Cars whipped past me, their drivers leaning on their horns. I was going only about forty miles per hour, but the cutout was bouncing up and down with a frightening amount of force.

Then I heard a "thwap" noise. One, two, three times. It wasn't the sound of the heavy cardboard violently hitting the car. It was a strange whipping noise, and every time it happened, I felt the cutout offer up a little less wind resistance.

I looked in the rearview and realized that pieces of the cutout were tearing off from their 3-D perches and flying through the air behind my car. An evil cartoon cat tore loose and went whizzing to my left. Moments later, an iron glove peeled away and flew off to my right.

Then, a third piece went hurtling straight back. It was a metal gear with Matthew Broderick's face on it. I watched as it flipped through the air—cardboard gear, Broderick head, cardboard gear, Broderick head, cardboard gear, Broderick head—over and over until, finally, it landed Broderick-head-down on the windshield of the police car that had pulled up behind me.

"Pull over right now," the trooper said into his loudspeaker. He didn't even bother to turn on his lights or siren.

I rolled to a halt on the shoulder of Route 18. The cop pulled up next to me and rolled his window down. Mine was already down, as I couldn't close it with the thick swatches of homemade rope ensnaring my car. The officer looked at me from his driver's seat, his eyes glancing from my face to the *Gadget* cutout to the yards of plastic. He shook his head and held up his hands.

Then he asked me a question that was totally fair.

"Are you fucking stupid?"

I didn't know what to say. So I went with honesty.

"Well, I work at Loews," I answered. He nodded his head in understanding.

He told me to throw everything away into the dumpster of the apartment complex we'd pulled over next to. He shook his head one more time before driving away. He didn't even give me a ticket. It would have been like kicking a three-legged dog.

I did as the officer said. It took me close to ten minutes to tear apart all the rope and hoist the cutout into a dumpster. The entire time, a confused housewife watched from her apartment window up above. I quit my job at Loews shortly after. For many years, the *Mumford* poster hung in my kitchen, a reminder of what I went through and how good it felt to escape. The scars of the horrible indignities and atrocities I participated in and witnessed at Loews are with me to this day. Wherever he is, I'm sure that Rhoderick understands.

Breaking Up, Breaking Down

Losing your mind is actually pretty fun when it leads to things like police chases and fistfights.

You feel like a maniac, but in an exhilarating daredevilish sort of way. This is the side of manic depression that's hard to realize is a problem: the manic side. That's the side that makes you wander down an abandoned boardwalk in Asbury Park, New Jersey, carrying an envelope containing close to $3,000 cash just to see what happens. It's the side that makes you participate in a rap battle circle you randomly stumble into by yourself near the West Side Highway in Manhattan at four in the morning on a Wednesday night. It's the side that makes you write a one-act play called "Time Phone" in less than fifteen minutes, and try to convince your friends to perform it that night in the ATM annex of a closed local bank.

It's fucked up to admit, but there's a part of me that didn't seek help for my manic depression because the manic side was pretty addictive. It made me feel daring, masculine, creative, and attractive to be around. The bottom line is that the manic side of manic depression is really fucking fun.

Of course, there's the other side of things, and that can catch up with you fast.

Veronica was the first to notice that my anxiety issues were overrunning my personality.

"Don't be nervous," she told me as we entered a party together. "Try not to do the thing where you rub your legs."

Veronica and I had grown pretty far apart by our junior year at Rutgers, but we were still dating. We'd developed two entirely different sets of friends. I rolled with a crew of dirtbag punk rock guys with nicknames like "Bonadooch," "Dirty Dave," and "The King of Coitus Interruptus." She'd linked up with a whole bunch of preppy musicians who were all current or former members of marching bands, loved to get together to jam out on their wood-winds, and redefined sweater-based fashion at Rutgers University.

We lived in different worlds. The difference was Veronica was able to adapt to mine. Sure, hanging out and drinking 40s of King Cobra malt liquor in a house that should have been condemned while listening to Screeching Weasel wasn't her cup of tea, but she was able to roll with the punches. On the other hand, when I was tasked with hanging out among her ilk, I shut down.

When conversations were at the most basic level, I'd be fine. I could answer questions like "How are you doing?" and "What is your major?" reasonably well. But as soon as those kids launched into discussions of what their favorite Sousa march was, I was socially crippled. I couldn't jump in with a joke. I couldn't ask a question to get them to explain what they were talking about. I couldn't even stay quiet and nod politely. As soon as I felt out of my element and in over my head, my lack of confidence would spiral out of control. The first warning sign that I was having an anxiety attack would be that I'd vigorously run my hands through my hair over and over again. Then I'd bite my nails one by one until I'd bitten all of them. Eventually I'd sit and rock back and forth. Rubbing my thighs was the final nail in the coffin, a sign that I was done for the evening. Once the thigh-rubbing phase of social anxiety had been achieved, I was unable to recover.

Veronica's gentle efforts to preempt my social meltdowns didn't help. Knowing the person I was closest to could see so clearly that I was falling apart only furthered the plummet in my self-esteem. While running around like a lunatic was fun and gave me cool stories, the rest of the time I was putting myself through hell. I'd go days without leaving my bedroom, skipping classes and avoiding friends. If anyone told me they thought I needed help, I'd find a way to cut them out of my life. I was backing myself into a corner with my own depression; I knew I needed help, but I was too scared to get it. And anyone who tried to make it happen became someone I feared.

Veronica, to her credit, stuck by me far longer than anyone should have. When I'd disappear for days on end, she'd accept my rambling apologies and excuses and try to move on. When I'd shut down in front of her friends and ignore her in front of mine, she did her best to accept it as a reflection of my growing problems and not as a judgment of her. And when I'd shut down completely, she'd quietly do her part to help get me back on my feet.

One of her main ways of taking care of me was making sure I was eating. Veronica would show up each afternoon with a slice of pizza from Ta Ta's, the bizarre restaurant across from my house on Hamilton Street. We'd sit together in silence, usually watching reruns of *Beverly Hills 90210* on cable, as I sadly ate. Often that would be the only thing I ate all day.

The fact that I owed my existence to Ta Ta's said it all. Because if there was any individual on earth who could unquestionably be deemed sad, it was old man Ta Ta, who burned through his days in a small pizza shack, a large metal oven four feet behind him, doling out slices to drunk, mean college kids. Ta Ta and his wife spent all day every day confined to that tin heat box, and going there as often as we did, my friends and I saw Ta Ta show signs of cracking on numerous occasions.

Once while I waited for a slice, Ta Ta received an order and dispatched his delivery boy. "You go to the side door of this house," he said. The delivery boy looked at him in confusion. Ta Ta's eyes grew wide with terror.

"Be careful," he continued. "This is a very scary house."

On another occasion, my friend Mike entered and Ta Ta was inside alone, crying behind the counter.

"Ta Ta, what's the matter?" Mike asked.

"It's nothing," Ta Ta answered. "I just found out my village in France has been destroyed by a flood. I'm waiting to hear if my brother is alive. What can I get you today?"

And yet, even this self-imprisoned sad sack was a step above me on the ladder of sanity, a veritable rock of stability in comparison. After all, my girlfriend could always count on stopping by his place for a slice on her way to my place to help me hold things together.

Eventually, though, not even a saint like Veronica could put up with me.

All throughout growing up as an angry little kid I'd managed to find a small sliver of hope in the form of comedy. I was obsessed with David Letterman, Andy Kaufman, Eddie Murphy, and *Saturday Night Live*. I consumed episodes of *Kids in the Hall* voraciously, and soaked up *Mystery Science Theater 3000* religiously.

Just as things were crumbling around me during my junior year, comedy provided me with hope again. It was during this time that I found the Upright Citizens Brigade Theater in Manhattan, a grungy comedy space housed in a former strip club on Twenty-second Street in Chelsea. As soon as I found it, I fell in love. There were shows every night of the week, and often they were free or five bucks. Most of the shows were hilarious and bizarre, and all of them were interesting on some level. And all of the performers were weirdos just like I was, a lot of them not that much older than me. Once I signed up for classes at the UCB, for the first time in a long time I felt like I had a home and a focus. Every weekend I'd head up to the city, hang out with people I felt connected to, enjoy the opportunity it provided me to be creative, and then get back on the train to New Brunswick.

Of course, the mere fact that this outlet was great for me didn't make it any easier to be around me. If anything, in addition to being a salvation, UCB gave me another place to hide, a way to put even more distance between myself and the person who wanted to help me the most.

After many years of watching me unravel and refuse help along the way, my high school sweetheart had finally had enough. One morning I was getting dressed before heading to the city when my phone rang. It was Veronica.

"When you get home today, don't make any other plans," she instructed me. "We have to talk about some stuff."

My stomach dropped.

"I get it," I said. "I'll call you when I'm back in town."

I headed to the train station, my head spinning. Veronica was going to break up with me. It had been a long time coming, and I knew I'd forced her hand. But still, this was the girl who had seen me grow up, had helped me do so, and now she was done with me. It was overwhelming. I didn't even have the energy to glare at The Worst Guy Ever when he came by asking for money.

The Worst Guy Ever wore a children's cancer hospital T-shirt and walked around the train station soliciting for money. The first time I saw him, I gave him a dollar. My older friends then told me that he had nothing to do with a kids' hospital and instead pocketed all the money. The next time he hit me up, I gave it to him.

"I know your scam and I think it's fucked up," I told him. "You're not getting any more money from me." I got on the escalator in the middle of the train station.

As I floated upward, he shouted "HEY!" I stopped and turned. I was the only one on the escalator. The entire train station heard the commotion and turned to watch.

"You," he said, "are a fucking faggot."

After that incident, whenever I was at the New Brunswick station and The Worst Guy Ever came by, I'd stare him down icily. He'd either remember me and scurry away or would engage and I'd tell him off again. But on a day like this, I didn't have it in me. Instead, I kept my head down and thought about how by the end of the day I wouldn't have a girlfriend.

I'd spent $12.50 on my round-trip train ticket. When I got to Penn Station, I bought my usual weekend-afternoon-in-the-city meal, an Auntie Anne's pretzel with nacho cheese dipping sauce. I had about five bucks left when I headed to my class.

After class, my fellow students started making plans. Usually we'd either go out drinking or watch a comedy show together. Normally, I was one of the guys leading the charge.

"Not this time," I told them. "I've gotta get back to Jersey so I can get dumped."

Some people made jokes. Others got awkward. One girl in my class approached me.

"I'm so sorry," she said.

"It's okay," I answered. "I deserve it."

I trudged back to Penn Station. There was a shitty flower stand in the main hall. I had five measly bucks left but figured Veronica deserved some sense of class from me, considering the situation. I bought a wilting red rose and headed to the main terminal to wait for my train.

If you ever need proof of the discrimination held against the state of New Jersey, pay a comparative visit to the two main train terminals in Manhattan. On the one hand, Grand Central Station is beautiful. That's where the trains to Westchester and Connecticut go. Everything's made of marble. People go there just to read because it's so peaceful. There's a farmer's market in the basement. The station even has an actual oyster bar.

I would *never* eat oysters at Penn Station. I wouldn't eat at the Nathan's Hot Dogs in Penn Station. I wouldn't eat food I bought somewhere else and brought inside Penn Station; once inside, that food instantly becomes garbage. If you ever walk through Penn Station, I invite you to note how the floor is always slightly moist. I can only assume this is the accumulative residue of many people's tears. God help anyone who has to use the men's room at Penn Station; there are people inside who can only be described as "lurkers."

It all adds up to the fact that on a normal day, Penn Station is a pretty soul-crushing place. On a day when I was waiting for a train to carry me back to the first true dumping of my young life, it was indescribable.

And yet, once I got on the Northeast Corridor train that night and sat down, an immense wave of relief washed over me. Because I knew how much of a fucking handful I was. As sad as breaking up would be, at least I knew I would no longer be subjecting someone I loved to dealing with it. Veronica would be better off. After all, I'd never had the guts to get help. I'd lied about it—said I was in the process of looking or acted like things were fine—until people stopped asking. Throughout it all, I'd used Veronica for support and forced her to put up with my bullshit when it served me. I was sad she was dumping me because I loved her, but I also recognized it was a good thing for her to move on, and as a result, during that train ride I became more calm and relaxed than I had been in months.

So much so that I fell asleep.

I woke up in Princeton Junction, one stop beyond the New Brunswick station.

I leapt off the train, moments away from being stuck onboard for a trip all the way to Trenton. For a moment, I stood on the Princeton platform alone. Snow was falling, I was holding a shitty rose, and I didn't have a dime in my pocket. (This was about two years before every single person in America simultaneously bought cell phones and made nights like this nonexistent.)

I ran into the station in a panic. Aside from a bored woman sitting behind the ticket counter, the station was desolate.

"I fell asleep," I said. "I'm supposed to be in New Brunswick."

"A one-way ticket to New Brunswick is five twenty-five," she told me.

"I have no money," I said. She grimaced. "Honestly. Zero dollars, zero cents."

She sighed.

"Look, the best I can say is get on the train on the other side of the platform and work it out with the conductor," she told me. "I won't bust you, but he might. Best I can do."

"Thanks," I said. When I looked back at her I had to fight back tears. Outside of the general stress of the day, it killed me that I had somehow managed to be an asshole to Veronica one last time. After all my disappearing acts and last-minute cancellations and generally evasive shitty behavior, I was going to be late for our fucking breakup.

I crossed over to the other side of the platform. At one end was a streetlight. I stood beneath it, hoping the light would give me a little bit of warmth to combat the cold, but it didn't.

After a few minutes, the ticket taker emerged on my side of the platform. She carried a broom and dustpan. She slowly made her way from the platform's entrance toward me, sweeping up along the way. As she got close, she bashfully smiled.

"You know," she said, "I think you're going to make some young lady very happy tonight."

I was confused. She looked down toward the rose.

"Oh," I said. "Not this time. Not tonight."

She was confused.

"It's not that kind of rose," I mumbled. My voice broke at the end. Before she knew what was happening, I was full on crying. Her face displayed a mixture of confusion, guilt, and slight fear. Luckily for both of us, the train pulled up and I got on.

The conductor didn't charge me. Half an hour later, Veronica broke up with me in her dorm room. Then, she drove us to a diner. We talked and she laughed a bunch; it reminded me of how things had been when we still felt like friends.

~~~

Two years later, I had a single night that changed my life.

It was a Friday, and I was scheduled to perform in a midnight show. My character was a Japanese schoolgirl, a living anime character, and my costume consisted of a skirt, a neon-yellow wig, huge googly-eyed glasses, and panty hose. When I saw myself in the green-room mirror, I started trembling.

You, I thought to myself, *look like a fucking idiot. Is this what you're working so hard for?*

Out of nowhere, I burst out crying. People backstage asked me what was wrong, but I didn't have the energy to answer. I actually did the show crying the whole time. Luckily the googly-eyed glasses masked my breakdown from the audience, but I freaked the shit out of my castmates.

As soon as the show was over I got the hell out of there. There was no traffic in the Lincoln Tunnel, so I made it to the Jersey side of the river in minutes. But being close to home didn't calm me down. I was still bawling.

I pulled over on the bridge on Route 3 that spans the Hackensack River.

I should get out and jump, I thought to myself. *Nah, it's not even high enough to do the job.*

Once I realized what I was thinking I cried even harder. Because I knew I really meant it. I wanted out.

Even though we hadn't spoken in over a year, I dialed the only number I could think of.

It was 2:30 A.M. She didn't owe me anything. But Veronica picked up after one ring.

"What's wrong?" she asked.

For the first time, I put all my cards on the table. I told her how my thoughts were running out of control. How sometimes I would make decisions that I actively knew were dangerous and had no idea why I did it. How I was giving up.

She talked to me for an hour while I made random turns through random suburban neighborhoods so I wouldn't have to go home. Once I was calm, she gave it to me straight.

"The entire time we were dating, you said you were going to get help," she began. "And you never did. But you need it."

"I know," I said. "I know."

"I can't be getting calls like this in the middle of the night, Chris," she continued. "So here's what's going to happen. When you get home tonight, you're going to wake your mother up and tell her what's going on. I'm going to call her in the morning. So if you haven't told her by then, I'm going to."

She was giving me no choice. It was exactly what I'd needed for years.

That night, I calmly woke my mother up from a sound sleep and told her I was in trouble. When she saw the state I was in, she asked me if I was suicidal. I told her that I thought I was.

"Do you think we should commit you to a mental hospital?" she asked me.

"I honestly don't know," I said.

We sat up for a few hours debating the merits of whether or not she should institutionalize me. It was one of the most surreal, fucked-up conversations of my life. In the end, we opted not to. Instead she sat next to me while I slept, keeping an eye on me.

The next morning I scheduled an appointment with a shrink. I'd hit rock bottom, but the people who loved me—even one I'd blown it with years before—helped me hold it together.

For the first time in a long time, I thought things might turn out okay.

No Worries

With the exception of a five-month stint in Los Angeles, I've spent my entire life living in New Jersey and Queens, and it shows. I am a stereotypical northeasterner. I'm always in a rush. I've attracted stares from out-of-towners when I've shoved past someone blocking the subway door. I've considered kicking a man's crutches out from under his feet because I thought he was going to make me late. It's not like I think this behavior is okay. It's just that I've spent more time sitting in Lincoln Tunnel traffic than most kids spend in front of the TV.

For a full six months after entering therapy, I felt shell-shocked and alone. I'd been put on medication, and was experiencing an array of side effects. Some were funny (Depakote made me fall asleep at the dinner table in the middle of a date); others were chilling (the muscle relaxant that accompanied my Risperdal warned of possible sexual side effects; I never dreamt that meant I would ejaculate what was for all intents and purposes water). It wasn't easy, but after a lifetime of anger, and a college career that only saw me grow more and more out of control, for the first time

I'd decided to get help and try to heal. I gave up drinking. I made it a point to actively search for the positive side of everything.

And perhaps as a result, after years of self-doubt and self-destructive behavior, I was finally dropping all of my internal defenses and starting to look at all the possibilities life offered.

So despite my loyalty and devotion to New Jersey, despite my long-standing job at *Weird NJ*, and despite the fact that it was the only home I'd ever known, when Matt Besser, the owner of the Upright Citizens Brigade Theater, called me in January of 2004 about a writing job for the Comedy Central show *Crossballs* (which he was executive producing), I knew I had no choice.

"I read your submission packet," he began. "You're not going to be a writer for my show, Chris."

I was let down. "That's okay, Matt. Thanks for giving me a shot."

"I'm not done," he interrupted. "I know you write for your magazine. And I know you're funny. So if you want to come out here and be a writers' assistant, I promise you that by the end of it, I will teach you how to write comedy."

I didn't hesitate. "Yes," I told him. "I'll do it."

"This job will not be glamorous," he told me. "And it will not be easy."

"That's okay," I told him. "I know how to work hard."

"Then be at work Monday, in LA," he told me. It was late on Thursday.

It was my first real job in entertainment and I was nervous, scared, and excited. But despite my anxiety, I was actually more than happy to make the move to the West Coast. I imagined that in addition to being a good career opportunity, it would provide me with not just a change of setting but a change in attitude, a fresh start. Los Angeles could be my own Shangri-la, a place where I could let my guard down. Relax. Give the veins in my forehead a break for a while. So with that one phone call I decided to drop my entire life in exchange for this chance at a new, less stressful beginning.

I spent my last weekend in New Jersey moving everything I owned from my apartment in Montclair to my parents' basement a few towns away. When I took the mirror down off of my closet door, I realized for the first time that I no longer looked like a kid. I was about to turn twenty-four. The boyishness that had plagued me throughout high school and college was quickly fading away. I had finally put on some weight (although that was actually just another unfortunate side effect of the Depakote). I certainly wasn't stylish, but it seemed as though taking care of myself had resulted in a happy by-product: for the first time in my life, I looked presentable.

At the bottom of a box I packed away the skunk my grandpa once tormented me with and the top hat I wore as White Magic. The framed covers of the *Weird NJ* issues I had worked on joined them. As I taped the last of the boxes shut, I sat on the edge of my bed and started to cry. Not because I was sad. And not really because I was happy. But because I realized that after twenty-two strange, hard years of willing insanity and one tough year of recovery, the roughest patch of my life was over.

The next morning my mom gave me a hug and helped me put my bags into a cab, and then I moved on.

~~~

I arrived way too early for my first day of work to find the doors to our bungalows locked. After five minutes of standing outside, I noticed a woman on a bike riding toward me. I assumed she was the first coworker I was meeting. I smiled and nodded to greet her. She skidded out on her bike. "If you nod at me again," she said, "I will fucking kill you." Then she rode away.

Welcome to Los Angeles. Welcome to your new life.

Most of the people I met in LA, even if they weren't completely crazy, unfortunately weren't much better than that girl on her bike. The majority of them were despicable in ways I consider worse than the most terrible aspects of New Yorkers. New Yorkers will be rude, but at least they do so out of the rationale that everyone around them is always slowing them down. Los Angeles, I learned, is a city full of people who have the personality of the coolest pretty boy from your eighth-grade class.* But I also met people who were a huge exception to this rule. They were all Mexicans.

The second day at my job, as I was walking across the lot I saw two production guys standing around a boom box that was blasting Morrissey. As a sad, angry teen, I'd grown to love Morrissey and was shocked to see that these tough Mexican guys did as well.

"You guys dig Moz?" I asked.

"Yeah, man," a shifty-looking guy said. "You wanna hit this?" He reached a lit joint toward me.

"No," I said, "we're at work."

"Little bitch," he said. "That's your name now. Little bitch. I'm Gomez. But you call me Padrino, 'cause I'm your godfather. That's Muerto." He pointed to his grinning friend.

"Doesn't that mean 'death'?" I asked. They both burst out laughing.

"Yeah," Gomez replied. "You'll see why."

---

*Also, they're pussies about driving in the rain.

I later used that interaction as an excuse to talk to Wendy, the cute receptionist I already had a crush on.

"What's Jose's deal?" I asked her.

"No one really knows," she answered. "All I know is that he has a side business where he drives shitty cars to Mexico and sells them every weekend. I have no idea how he gets back to work every Monday."

I grinned at her, hoping she would grin back and we could start a love affair that would end in our happy marriage. She did not.

"Why do they call him 'Muerto'?" I asked.

"It's hard to explain," she told me.

It didn't take me long to find out how Jose earned his nickname. Just a few days later, while walking down a hallway, I was blindsided and tackled to the floor. Jose cackled as he pinned me down. He reached down to my jeans, sticking his fingers deep into a small hole in the knee. "Who's the king?" he asked me.

"What?" I answered.

With that he tore my entire left pant leg to shreds. He leapt to his feet, cackling again as he sprinted away. I spent the rest of the workday enduring jokes about my eviscerated pants, which looked like they belonged on some old-timey pirate.

Gomez and Jose's favorite activities seemed to be: (1) smoking weed; (2) sleeping; (3) playing basketball; and (4) telling me long-winded stories about how they were forced into being drug mules during their teenaged years. Despite the fact that work isn't on that list, they also managed to do their jobs, and well, too. But as far as my personal interactions with them went, anyway, they were usually involved in one of these four things.

Hear me out, though. I'm not saying that my Mexican friends were lazy. I don't believe in that stereotype. These guys produced an enormous amount of effort. It's just that they aimed all of their effort at being laid-back and having fun. There's a difference between that and laziness. Lazy people spend their time sitting on Facebook or yelling at racist fifteen-year-olds who are also playing the newest version of "Call of Duty." These Mexican guys didn't waste time like that. What they demonstrated wasn't laziness; it was aggressive relaxation. I even hoped that one day I could learn to live like them. They were the first people I'd met who lived with such a little amount of anxiety. Considering how I'd spent a quarter century being nothing but stressed out, it's understandable how I quickly came to idolize my two new friends.

Gomez took the idea of being laid-back to a whole new level. He summed it up with two simple words—"No worries." There was nothing you could say to phase Gomez. And if you came close, "No worries" was the magic phrase that drained all the tension back out of the room. During one particularly tough shooting day, all of our props were late to set. I panicked, tried to rectify the situation, and turned to Gomez for help.

"Gomez," I said, "you think we can get that stuff here by four o'clock?"

"What'd you call me, you little bitch?" he said in his slow drawl.

"Gomez, we—" He interrupted me.

"What?" He grinned.

"*Mi Padrino*, do you think we can get that stuff?"

"No worries," he said. "You little bitch."

No worries. This was Gomez's defining philosophy on life. It was his mantra, his guiding principle. And he never deviated.

I tried to adopt this philosophy as my own, but it was slow going. When the company that shipped my car from New Jersey took close to a month to deliver it instead of the week they'd promised, I said *No worries* to myself. But it didn't stop me from being furious. When the car arrived and was strangely coated in a thick layer of rock-salt residue, I again told myself *No worries*. I still wanted to punch the truck driver in the face. *No worries* was easy to say, but the mind-set was hard to adopt. You can take the nebishy, neurotic, hyperbolically angry kid out of the Northeast, but that doesn't mean he's going to be anything other than nebishy, neurotic, and hyperbolically angry somewhere else, I guess.

When Gomez strolled into my office one Wednesday afternoon while Jose blocked the doorway, I knew something was about to happen, and that it was most definitely trouble. *No worries*, I tried to tell myself. *No worries*.

"Little bitch," Gomez said, a slight smirk on his face.

"What's up, Padrino? I'm kind of busy," I replied in the shitty tone that is my trademark when I'm stressed.

"What are you doing this weekend?" he asked.

"Nothing, I don't know, why?" I snorted.

"Don't make plans." He grinned. "We're taking you to TJ."

TJ. Tijuana. Before I could protest, he walked off. Muerto followed behind, his trademark cackle at full volume.

Tijuana would have intimidated me even if I weren't being led around by a former drug mule who thought of me as his bitch. As someone who had just stopped drinking eighteen months earlier and who was finally feeling good about himself, I was scared shitless at the prospect of heading to a debaucherous party city of terrifying proportions. And yet I didn't protest. I didn't bitch or moan. It turns out I wanted to go. I figured if I was going to leave New Jersey for California, I might as well extend the adventure and check out Mexico. Besides, I had to push myself. A big part of my motivation to move had been to try something new, something beyond the familiarity in which I had lived for so many years. Coming to Los Angeles had been a good first step that I had taken on my own—but in my quest to relax, it was the Mexicans who set the bar for me. Maybe going to Mexico would show me how they managed to pull it off.

Besides, for all their crazy behavior, Gomez and Jose were my friends. If they wanted to show me where and how they grew up, I was not going to say no. *No worries*, I told myself.

We left after work on Friday and the trip quickly developed an uneasy air about it. Jose picked me up in an old, broken-down white van, undoubtedly part of his underground car-sale empire. "Get in, pussy," he said as he screeched to a halt. He was driving with one hand and rolling a joint with the other.

I climbed inside. We stopped for gas just a few blocks from work. Since the car's gas gauge was broken, the automatic cutoff didn't work and Jose sprayed about four gallons of gasoline all over the ground. He climbed back into the driver's seat.

"Dude," I said, "we gotta tell someone. They've gotta clean that up."

"No worries," he replied.

"But Jose, someone could light a cigarette and torch this place," I protested.

"No worries, you little bitch," he said. We drove away.

Jose lit his joint five minutes after we got onto the highway. A slight contact high set in as we headed deeper into Southern California than I'd ever been. The desert rolled into the distance on either side of the highway and I realized that I'd never seen anything like it in my entire life. I rolled down the window and put my feet up on the dashboard. By the time we cruised past the San Diego skyline, I was as relaxed as I'd been in about half a decade. Finally, Southern California was having an effect on me. Jose smoked nonstop until we came to the border, and not even the manic bustle of the crossing managed to stress me out.

We pulled up in front of Gomez's house and my Padrino jumped in the car.

"We gotta show you the town, little bitch," Gomez said. "Let's go to the bar."

"I don't drink," I told them.

"No worries," they said in unison. We parked downtown and entered a bar called Adelita's. It looked nice, almost like a club. As we entered, I realized that its niceness was a moot point, and that the major difference between this bar and others was actually the prostitutes. The hundreds of prostitutes. Women in bikinis, women in lingerie, women in street clothes. They wandered all around Adelita's. Big ones, little ones, light ones, dark ones, ugly ones, and yes, beautiful ones.

"Yo, you little bitch," Gomez said to me. "You can fuck any of these women for forty dollars. Which one you want?"

"I don't want to sleep with a hooker," I said, very seriously. "Get me out of here."

Jose started to protest.

"No," I said. "Get me out of here. Right now."

Gomez was irritated. "All right, no worries!" he said, bristling at my anger.

We shuffled outside, not talking. Jose grabbed the van and pulled up in front of the bar. We jumped in, and Muerto dropped us off at Gomez's house shortly after. He soon left, presumably to go sell that piece of shit van.

Gomez and I got food before heading to his family's home. The streets surrounding it were narrow and busy, filled with people and honking cars. But when he lifted the large metal garage door that marked the border of his property, I was shocked to see a beautiful estate. I stepped onto a large stone patio, vegetables growing around its border, and Gomez's lovely mother ran out to meet us and hugged me immediately. We sat outside on lounge chairs, looking out over the city. I met Panchi, Gomez's Chihuahua, who, Gomez informed me, had a huge dick. "Sometimes I wake up in the morning, and he's running around, dragging it on the ground behind him," he told me. "Whenever that happens and you catch him, he looks at you, and he always looks real ashamed."

I laughed. After our showdown at the bar, I feared that Gomez and I would be at odds. But a meal and some bizarre stories had gotten us back to business as usual. I looked at the tiny (but huge) dog and laughed again. Gomez grinned at me.

"Now, look," he said, "do you want to go back and get a hooker or what?"

"Dude, no!" I exploded. I was amazed he brought it back up after our earlier blowout. "And I'm really not sure why you won't just drop this."

Disappointed, I opted to head to bed rather than hang out with my Padrino any longer. I woke up at three in the morning to Gomez shaking me.

"Little bitch," he said. "Little bitch, wake up."

"What's wrong?" I asked. I imagined nightmarish scenarios where the drug runners who forced Gomez into mule-itude had returned and were now after me.

"Nothing. But look, let's go back to Adelita's," he said. "You can fuck a whore. I won't tell anyone, not even Muerto."

I looked up at Gomez, my friend. In the short time I'd known him he'd already shown me a lot and I appreciated him for it. Still, enough was enough. I felt the familiar sensation of anger snapping to life inside me. Since moving to California I'd come to enjoy a sunny rage-free few months, but now, with Gomez's late-night prostitution prodding, it returned. I sat up, and though I was still half asleep, I lost my cool. I pounded my fist into the bed and gave Gomez a wild-eyed stare.

"Gomez," I said. "Look at me. I'm gonna tell you one more fucking time, and then we're going to have a serious fucking problem. *I don't want to fuck a whore.*"

"Why not, man?" he said. His voice melted from insistence to desperation. "It's clean. They even give you a towel afterward."

"What do you think my problem with this is?" I shouted. "And why do you think a towel will fix it?"

"Damn you, little bitch," he yelled. "You gotta get it over with sometime."

I rolled over. He stayed in the room. I ignored him—if I hadn't, we would have wound up in a full-on shouting match or, worse yet, a fistfight. Lying on my bed in furious silence I kept hearing one phrase, rolling over and over in my head—*"Get it over with sometime."*

Get what *over with sometime?* I asked myself. I'd never seen Gomez this insistent about anything, nor this upset. *Get* it *over with sometime?* I repeated it in my head. *It?*

Then it hit me. I sat straight up in bed and turned to my friend.

"Gomez, do you think I'm a virgin?"

He blinked. "You're not?"

For the first time, I saw myself as my new friends did.

When high-strung Americans see laid-back Mexicans, they tend to unfairly label them as lazy. It occurred to me that when Mexicans see someone as high-strung as me, someone always in a rush, someone always irritated, they must make assumptions, too. In this case, the only logical explanation for a person who behaved like me was that he must have never gotten laid in his entire life.

I breathed heavily, unsure of what to think. *Okay,* I told myself, *you're twenty-four years old and they think you're a virgin. That's humiliating.*

But I was also touched. For much of my life I'd felt like I'd had to fight every battle on my own. Now an immense sense of gratitude overtook me as I realized that Gomez wasn't mocking me. He was looking out for me. Misguided and embarrassing, yes, but the important thing was I had a friend who had the heart to treat me to a Tijuana whore.

I looked at Gomez, his sleepy eyes waiting for an answer. I wanted to express myself, but couldn't find the words. How did I explain that I was angry, but also touched? And that I wasn't what he thought I was? Finally, I said the one thing I knew would get across everything I was feeling. For the first time, it made sense.

"Padrino," I said, grinning at him. "No worries."

"My boy!" Gomez yelled, probably waking up his big-dicked dog. "For real?"

I nodded. Without saying anything else, he understood.

Since that trip, Gomez has stopped calling me "little bitch." Now, he calls me "Padrinito"—the little godfather.

A few short months later, *Crossballs* wrapped. I didn't have another job lined up and debated whether to stay or to head home to the Northeast. On the one hand, there was Los Angeles, a place I had just begun scratching the surface of, a place that had afforded a necessary reboot of my personality, but one that also, I sensed, was overall too gilded and superficial for my liking.

On the other hand, there were New Jersey and New York. Places I had deep connections to and very fond memories of, but places that I had some long-standing and still painful negative associations with.

Early in the summer of 2004, I made up my mind and drove cross-country back home. I owed the East Coast another shot. I'd never known it while I was happy. I'd never experienced it with *No worries.*

Six Red Bumps

"I thought you had my back!" I shouted into Allison's face as we stood next to an Italian sausage stand. "It's my mistake for making such a stupid assumption."

"Will you calm down?" she pleaded. "I didn't realize this was a whole-day thing!"

"I didn't realize," I said, "I was dating someone who cared so little about me."

~~~

Being angry with someone you love is terrible. But converting the passion of that anger into sexual acts is a euphoric experience that I can't recommend enough. Makeup sex is absolutely the best sex you can have.

A few Labor Day weekends ago, my girlfriend Allison and I went to the Jersey Shore. The Shore's perfect for us; Allison loves the beach and I love deep-fried Oreos. And both of us love looking at mulleted weirdos in airbrushed tank tops who get drunk in the afternoon.

We relaxed, swam, and shared as terrific a meal as one can find on a boardwalk. We rode through a cheesy haunted house and laughed when a fat man smoking a cigarette jumped out from the darkness.

Although we had been dating only a few months, I realized that we were experiencing our first perfect day together, and as we walked among the lights and sounds and games, I began to suspect I really loved the girl.

Then Allison's phone rang.

"Hey, Clair," she said, turning her back to me. "Maybe eight or nine? No, put me on the list," she said. Allison placed her hand over the receiver. "What time do you think we're getting back tonight?" she asked.

"I don't know," I said. Then, I walked away. She caught up to me in front of a store that sold T-shirts with phrases about Italian people on them. My fists were balled.

"Are you okay?" she asked.

"Why did you ask what time we're getting back?" I snapped at her.

"There's a party," she said. "I thought maybe we could get back in time for it."

"I can't believe this fucking bullshit," I said. Anger, my old friend, had returned.

I felt stupid, ashamed I had spent the past few hours thinking this was "our first perfect day" while, in the meantime, Allison obviously couldn't wait to leave and was already planning her night out without me. I took it to mean that all of my cheesy romantic thoughts weren't being reciprocated, and being a boneheaded male unable to handle emotions I reverted to what was most familiar to me: I began to yell and curse.

"This is a big misunderstanding," she said. "I'm not trying to be mean."

"There's no misunderstanding," I said. "I'll just drive you home so you can hang out with the people you'd *rather* be with!"

"I want to be with *you*," Allison answered.

"You have a funny way of showing it," I snapped.

Our fight continued all the way back to the car and it didn't stop there. We yelled at each other on the Garden State Parkway, continued the yelling as we merged onto the New Jersey Turnpike, and waiting to get through the Holland Tunnel we killed some time with more yelling. Though we were far from the first people to scream in frustration while sitting in Tunnel traffic, I can guarantee we were some of the most committed. We kept at it as we pulled up in front of Allison's dorm. And then for good measure we yelled for another hour in my car, blocking traffic on Fourteenth Street.

"I didn't mean to insult you!" Allison said for the fiftieth time that night.

"Well, I'm having a tough time figuring that out," I continued. "Because when all you can think about is getting away from me, I find it pretty insulting."

"Chris, I'm sorry," Allison said. "I love you and I didn't mean to hurt you."

"I love you too," I said. "If I didn't, there's no way I could possibly get this mad."

And then, suddenly, after so many hours of arguing, it was gone. Exhausted, we finally began to calm down and really listen to each other.

"Do you want to come back to my place?" I asked.

"Yes," Allison said. "Yes, I do."

I've never driven through Manhattan that fast, nor have I weaved my way through the traffic on the Queensboro Bridge as skillfully. We were back at my apartment in no time flat, and when we got there we attacked each other.

I won't be cross. Suffice it to say that all that dark, brooding aggression fell by the bedside. And at one point a pineapple-flavored Marino's Italian Ice was involved. That part was cool.

~~~

The next morning I woke up first and for a moment watched Allison as she slept. Sunlight was streaming through the blinds and hitting her face. Allison is a petite girl, but when she's in a bed by herself, she spreads all of her limbs out to take up the entire mattress. It's adorable. I realized that I had been a moron the day before at the Shore. I had been hurt, but my reaction to that pain had led to a horrible day that risked our relationship. It was inexcusable. The amount of jealousy I felt at being snubbed for Allison's friends was nothing compared to the hurt I created in response.

Allison rolled over and mumbled. I smiled. It was a perfect start to the morning.

A perfect start that immediately came to an end when I went into the bathroom and peed. That's when I sensed a strange, pulsating feeling emanate from the tip of my penis. It wasn't a burning sensation, and it didn't quite hurt. It felt like someone had applied just a slight pressure between finger and thumb on the head of my dick. The initial shock was like driving a car you're familiar with and realizing that something is wrong with the transmission—the car was still running, but something was *off*.

I looked down and was horrified to see six red bumps forming a ring around my urethra. I sprinted back into my room and collided with my desk chair. Allison shot out of bed.

"We've got a problem," I said. I motioned wildly toward my penis.

The beginning of my morning had been idyllic. Allison's was off to a much rockier start. She leaned in close to examine the ring of raised red blotches on my junk.

"What the hell is that?" she said, eyes wide with fear.

"I don't fucking know," I said.

"Was that there when we—"

I interrupted her.

"Fuck no it wasn't there," I said. "There's no way I wouldn't have felt it. It feels like my dick is trapped underneath a dictionary."

I grabbed the camera case hanging from the doorknob of my closet.

"I'm going to take pictures of the bumps," I told her.

"Why the fuck would you do that?" she shouted at me.

"What if they go away? I need to show a doctor," I said.

I didn't know what else to do. I had never been in this situation before. The only thing remotely close was the time my first girlfriend had a pregnancy scare after the second time we had sex. But I'd since discovered that everyone's first girlfriend has a pregnancy scare after the second time they have sex. This was something else entirely. There was only one thing I knew for sure—I had to see a doctor.

"What do we do?" Allison asked. "You don't have health insurance."

It was true, I didn't. A proper doctor's visit would have emptied my savings account.

"I'll have to go to a health clinic," I said.

I knew many friends who had returned from clinics with war stories. Based on their accounts, I could only assume I was about to enter some sort of medical purgatory, with all the impersonal

interactions of a hospital and none of the modern-day equipment. Worse yet, it was Labor Day. There wasn't a single clinic
open in the five boroughs of New York City. I would have to wait
an entire day before I could find out why there were six red
bumps on my penis.

In the meantime, naturally, my next step was to get on the
computer and self-diagnose on WebMD.

"Do you think it's that?" Allison asked as we sat in front of
my computer.

"It looks like it," I said. "But this hasn't existed since they
found antibiotics."

"Oh man," Allison said, "I hope you didn't bring back some
medieval shit."

When I was done hyperventilating I researched different
health clinics around the city. I found a city-run program in
Corona, just a few neighborhoods away from me in Queens. It
was open the next day and it was free. It was also dedicated
specifically to STDs. In the grip of fear, I believed it was the perfect place for me and my six red bumps.

In hindsight, I realize this was a huge mistake. If you ever
have any problem of any sort, let alone a medical problem, let
alone a medical problem involving your penis, Corona, in
Queens, is not where you should go to solve it. Nothing against
the neighborhood of Corona. It's just that when I think of top-
notch medical care in New York, I think of Mt. Sinai and New
York Presbyterian University hospitals. When I think of Corona,
I think of great Mexican food and good deals on storage space.

There's also the matter of getting what you pay for. When certain things are free it's cause for rejoicing. Free Internet access,
for example, makes me shout from the rooftops. I also absolutely
make it a point to grab a free Slurpee from 7-Eleven every July
11th, and the first time Burger King ran its "Free Fri-day" pro-

motion, I spent a night driving from Burger King to Burger King, claiming more than my share of deep-fried potatoes.

Sexually based medical care, on the other hand, probably shouldn't be placed in the same category as potatoes, slush, or wireless Internet.

It's easy to see all of this now. Unfortunately, one of the sad side effects of finding six red bumps on your dong is severely clouded judgment. Hence within forty-eight hours of discovering those bumps, I found myself sitting in the waiting room of a makeshift doctor's office in Corona.

The clinic was located in a former government building. At some point the board of education or neighborhood zoning committee had apparently found better digs and left the place to the wilds, until someone set up medical offices inside. I stood in the lobby, surrounded by desks and upside-down chairs. A handwritten sign pointed me toward STD testing.

I walked down a musty hall and pushed open a door. Around thirty-five people quietly sat in beat-up folding chairs. Thirty-one of them were native Spanish speakers. There was one other white guy, rubbing his knees and swaying in a way that can only be mastered after years of heroin abuse. There was also one cool-ass black guy who was there with two girls, both fawning over him.

You brought two girls to an STD clinic? I thought to myself. *That's the most baller thing I've ever seen.*

And then there was me, the wide-eyed kid in the Old Navy polo shirt. I scrambled to figure out how to say the words "six red bumps" in Spanish.

Six rouge tetons? I thought to myself. *No, that's French. And I think I would be telling the nurse that I have six red breasts.*

I sat in the waiting room for two hours. I hadn't brought a book, but luckily the clinic was screening the movie *Jumanji*. This normally wouldn't be a film in my wheelhouse. But it was the Spanish-language version, and there were no subtitles, so really I didn't have to watch it so much as I had the opportunity to watch 1995-level special effects unfold as characters shouted in a language I didn't understand. I received a series of text messages from Allison, but as far as distractions go they were more heartbreaking then entertaining.

"ARE YOU OKAY?"

"I LOVE YOU"

"SORRY WE HAD A FIGHT"

You know someone's freaked out, I told myself, *when even their text messages seem scared.*

I sat in the waiting room for hours. I was alone when a maintenance man began stacking chairs around me. Finally, the woman at the registration computer looked up at me in surprise.

"What number are you?" she asked.

"23," I mumbled.

"Oh! You slipped right through the cracks! Come in, come in!" she said.

I answered questions about my sexual history—number of partners, which parts of human bodies I had entered, which parts of mine other human bodies had entered, that sort of thing.

"You're in our system," she said. "So did you want to see a doctor, or is that all?"

It was then that I realized exactly how bad of a mistake I had made. Sitting for two hours in a free clinic was irritating but expected. Waiting two hours only to have someone then ask whether you showed up to actually see a doctor or simply to enter your personal contact information and entire sexual history into their computers set me off. *No need to hassle the doctor*, I wanted to say. *The data-entry portion of this process cleared up a lot of the worries I had. Now that I know you have my evening phone num-*

ber I feel a lot more secure about the red bumps that appeared all over my dick a few days ago.

Instead, because I am a coward who screams on kiddie roller coasters, I simply murmured, "Seeing a doctor would be great."

A few minutes later a small female Asian doctor looked around the empty waiting room and called out "Number 23!" I followed her into her office where she told me to drop my pants. Before my boxers hit the ground, she nonchalantly said, "Oh, you have herpes."

I froze. Herpes. The least desirable of all sub-AIDS STDs. Gonorrhea? That sucks, but at the end of the day it's just anti-biotics and a memorable story. Herpes is a lifelong nightmare. My jaw dropped.

"It's actually not bad," she told me. "Herpes really gets a bad rap." I wasn't sure what to say to that. Luckily, my face had gone numb as soon as I heard the word "herpes," so I was physically unable to speak anyway. Before I knew what was happening, an oversized cotton swab was being inserted up the shaft of my penis. "Just wait right here," she said. "We'll get your test results right now."

I was sent back into the waiting room. I sat for another hour, completely alone. *Jumanji* was on replay. A man finally approached me.

"Can I help you?" he asked.

"Yeah . . . I'm waiting for my test results," I weakly said.

"Oh, that's you? I finished that a while ago," he said. "Come with me." We went into his office. "I am happy to tell you that you are clean," he informed me. All the tension drained out of my body. "You don't have syphilis, gonorrhea, or chlamydia."

I was confused. "What about herpes?"

"Oh," he said, "we don't test for herpes here."

"But that's what the doctor thought I had," I told him.

"Well, we don't test for it here . . . ," he again explained.

"Then why did she shove a Q-tip up my dick hole?!" I shouted.

I stood up slowly, making sure to control myself so I didn't throw my chair across the room. I stomped out the door and marched back to my car. Once inside, I burst out crying. Then I did what I almost always do when I cry. I called my mom.

"Chris?" she asked as she picked up the phone. "Shouldn't you be at work?"

"Mom, I just got back from the doctor," I sobbed.

"What's wrong?" she asked, bracing for the worst.

"They think I have herpes," I said, breaking down as I said it.

There was a long pause. I sensed my mother was cycling through any number of possible responses.

"Maybe you shouldn't tell me things like that," she finally said. "Also, I think we might have a weird relationship."

I went home and broke the horrible news to Allison. I was crying, terrified that I had infected her with an STD I didn't know I had. To her credit, Allison was stronger than I was, and insisted I get a second opinion.

A few days later, I tracked down another clinic, one that charged a fee and was in Manhattan—two good signs. It was a facility aimed at providing low-cost medical care to gay men, but it didn't discriminate against heterosexuals and I don't discriminate against anyone at all, certainly not those who provide me with affordable health care.

While sitting in the lobby, I ran into a female acquaintance of mine.

"What are you doing here?" I asked as she waved hello.

"I volunteer here. What about you?" she asked.

"I'm here to . . . uh. . . . " I looked at the floor.

A nurse interrupted. "Mr. Get Hard, you can go to the fourth floor."

My acquaintance's face dropped. I looked on the wall and saw the words "Fourth Floor" and "STD Clinic" side by side. *Great,* I told myself, *she thinks I have AIDS.* I trudged to the elevator without saying another word to her. *Well,* I reminded myself, *much worse things have been said about me.*

"There were six of them," I told the doctor. "Raised a little bit. I have digital pictures if you want to see them."

"That's really okay," the doctor said, stopping me.

"Okay, okay," I said, nervously. "Thank you for, um, I mean—"

"Chris, you have nothing to be ashamed of," he said. "I'm a doctor at the biggest clinic in Chelsea. I've seen it all. Even if you have herpes, you can't imagine what a refreshing change of pace that is." It was nice to know that even if worst came to worst, at least I'd be able to help the doctor's day.

Then he produced a cotton swab that was even larger than the one the maniacal Asian lady had wielded.

"I just have to make sure," I said. "You do test for herpes here, right?"

"Yeah," he said. He gently violated me and said the results would take a few days.

Afterward, I met up with Allison, and was saddened to tell her that I again returned with no answers. We took the train back to my place. A dismal air had fallen over the both of us.

I slumped down, exhausted from running such a gauntlet of emotions over such a short period of time. I was completely burnt out.

I looked at Allison and smiled meekly. On the boardwalk she had seen me truly angry for the first time. Now on the subway, she was seeing me defeated. She put my head on her shoulder.

Moments later, she shoved my head out of the way and leapt out of her seat.

"Pineapple ice!" she shouted. I looked at her, utterly confused. "Pineapple ice!" she repeated, waiting for it to dawn on me.

Then I realized what she was getting at and I burst out laughing. The jaded New Yorkers surrounding us turned up their iPods and ignored our moment of elation. It all came back: The boardwalk. The fight. The ride home. The sex. The thing she did with the pineapple ice. We hugged and laughed.

A few days later, the doctor called me and verified her suspicions.

I'm relieved to say I have never had herpes, but I do have a skin allergy to FD&C Yellow #5.

Colonic

"The worst part of raising you," my mother recently told me, "was that you always had to go to the bathroom."

My father nodded. "I wanted to kill you almost all the time."

"Car trips were the worst," my mother said. "Every time we passed a rest stop, you forced us to pull over."

"And rest stops are filthy," my father continued. "Just disgusting." He shook his head, recalling the myriad unsanitary places his young son pooped in.

"I'm so glad," my mother said, "that you grew out of that."

I couldn't figure out the best way to correct her.

~~~

Doing diarrhea onto another person's hands is the sort of thing you don't know you want to do until you do it.

Recently, a stomach virus swept through New York City, and I caught it bad. The first symptom I noticed was that I couldn't go to the bathroom. Things got worse from there. Initially I was tired and out of sorts, but still able to go through my daily routine. I had decided to follow through on a scheduled visit to see my brother in Philadelphia when my body really went haywire. I was already pretty down and out by the time I got there, but halfway through the day, my sinuses blew up in a way I'd never experienced.

"Dude, you all right?" Gregg asked as we punched in our sandwich orders at WaWa. I used my sandwich-ordering console to prop myself up on my suddenly wobbly legs.

"I think my brain just exploded," I said.

I cancelled my order for a sub (or hoagie, as those with obnoxious Philly accents insist on calling them) and headed straight to my car.

On my way up the New Jersey Turnpike, I started experiencing cold sweats. By the time I reached that postapocalyptic-looking stretch of oil refineries near Elizabeth, I was positive a fever had set in. When I pulled up in front of my apartment in Queens, my head was spinning—or, rather, everything else was. I barely made it up the two flights of steps to my apartment. Even turning the key took a massive amount of effort, but I made it inside. I collapsed on the couch and stayed completely still for over an hour while the entire room revolved around me.

Finally, I summoned the will to call my mother.

"Mom," I said when she picked up, "I think—"

"Why are you calling this late?" she asked. "*Dancing with the Stars* is on."

"Mom, I think I'm dying," I wheezed.

"What's wrong?" she asked. I could tell that dancing celebrities were distracting her.

"My stomach's been going nuts for days," I said. "And today my sinuses went crazy and I have a headache. And I feel nauseous. Everything's spinning."

"Drink some Gatorade," she said.

"Gatorade?" I countered. "Mom, I'm dying here. Gatorade isn't gonna cut it. Should I walk up to Elmhurst Hospital?"

"What? Hospital?" she asked. "You don't go to hospitals for things like this. They'll just give you Gatorade anyway and charge you a thousand dollars for it."

"You're right," I said.

"Yeah," my mom replied. "You gotta learn to suck it up, Chris."

I hung up the phone and collapsed on the couch. I didn't wake up until late the next afternoon.

When I awoke, the traces of the suicide virus were seemingly gone. I no longer had a fever, I wasn't sweating uncontrollably, and I wasn't crying like a despicable coward. Unfortunately, there was a lingering problem related to the disease. I still could not go to the bathroom. To make it worse, I now constantly felt like I had to go to the bathroom.

This lasted for four excruciating days. That's ninety-six hours of feeling like I had to poo and not being able to pull it off. Five thousand seven hundred and sixty minutes of being constipated. On the rare occasion that I did manage to squeeze out some pitiful pebble, I would stand up and instantly feel like I had to go again. There was no relief in sight.

I can usually handle struggles relating to fecal matter. In fact, I'd classify myself as an expert. I come from a long line of irritable bowel syndrome–ridden Irish folks with bad stomachs and worse diets. I have shit my pants at least a dozen times during my adult life. Honestly, I can't recall making it through a year without shitting my pants at least once. If you count Hershey squirts and sharts, that number rises considerably.

But this—this was something I hadn't encountered before. I've had diarrhea and I've been constipated, but this was some terrible combination of the two—all the stomach pain and constant fear of losing control that accompanies diarrhea, with all

the frustration and hopelessness of constipation. Instead of can-
celing each other out, these were two negatives that fed off and
helped each other grow exponentially.

Something drastic had to be done. I had gone to all of my old
standbys. Salads weren't helping. Fiber did nothing. I had to take
it to the next level.

Clutching my midsection, I limped to a drugstore and looked
through all the different laxative options. I was well versed in the
ways of Ex-Lax and all the natural remedies, but my gut was
telling me that something more extreme was necessary. And by
that I mean my gut was shifting oddly inside my midsection and
making sounds that roughly emulated the mournful death tune
of a noble beached whale.

Among the options available at the drugstore was an enema.
I'd never used one before, which was something of a personal
point of pride. Unfortunately, the nonenema portion of my life
had come to a close. I didn't have any particular desire to shove
a plastic tube up my ass, but I knew it would have an effect.

I was right near my girlfriend's apartment. Allison wasn't
home, nor was her roommate, who is also her male cousin. I
knew she was occupied for the next few hours, and he was a
banker who worked around eighteen hours a day. Of course,
normally I wouldn't use anyone's home but my own for enema
administration, but the idea of sitting on a train back to my
place when relief was so close at hand was maddening. I giddily
made my way up the five flights of steps that led to Allison's
apartment knowing that salvation was within reach.

Once inside I went to the bathroom, lay on my side, inserted
a lubricated tube into my asshole, and squeezed a bulb full of
saline solution up into my rectum. I can't lie about it—I didn't
feel weird at all. I stayed on the ground for about five minutes,

tightly holding the liquid in my ass. The instructions recommended lying on my left side so that the solution might travel as far as possible up my intestinal tract. I did so, and could feel gravity sucking the goo deep into my insides. Those three or four minutes on the cool tile floor of my girlfriend's bathroom having just used her apartment as an enema station without her knowledge easily qualify as some of the most awkward minutes of my very awkward life.

The end result was worth it. Eventually I felt an overwhelming urge, so I stood up and leapt to the toilet. I took a satisfying bowel movement, my first in four days. Clouds parted and angels sang. I was a prisoner suddenly freed after decades behind bars, a soldier reunited at long last with a woman with whom he'd had a torrid love affair before the chaos of war had separated them. In that moment I lived these and every other cliché. If I wasn't shitting so hard, I would have dropped to my knees and shouted to the heavens.

After ten of the most glorious minutes of my life, I cleaned myself up, walked into Allison's living room, and put the used enema and its box into a plastic bag. I tied the bag shut and sealed it tightly. I wanted to leave quickly, but my body was feeling rocked from the physical exertion of expelling half a week's worth of shit.

I collapsed onto Allison's couch—at which point her roommate/cousin walked through the door, inexplicably accompanied by four fellow former members of the Cornell lacrosse team. My understanding of the banking industry had always been that they work young employees to the bone without exception. I guess they do allow workers to take half-days, but only when doing so will create a maximum level of awkwardness for all parties involved.

"Oh hey, Matt," I said, hoping he couldn't sense in my voice that I had recently violated myself. "Allison's not home. She said I could hang out here for. . . . " My voice trailed off as I tried to think of an excuse for being there without Allison.

"It's cool," he said. "We're going to watch the football game. I don't know if you'd want to join us, but you're more than welcome."

I felt them all looking at me, at the end of the couch. And I saw them glancing down at the plastic bag by my feet.

These were men's men, guys who worked in finance and dressed in shirts and ties. Apparently they had come from some sort of benefit. We were definitely from different worlds. They were well-dressed young athletes with Ivy League educations. I was a state-school graduate with no day job who had in his possession an empty plastic bulb coated in a film of his own shit. I would have felt uncomfortable around guys like this on a normal day. Being that five minutes prior I had been abusing myself with a plastic tube, my feelings of inadequacy were even more pronounced than usual.

"I don't know," I told Matt.

"Come on," he said, as welcoming as always. "Hang out a little bit."

"Sure," I mumbled.

After a quarter of rooting on a football team I did not care about, I told Matt that I had to get going and made my way to the door. I grabbed the remains of my enema and held the bag as far as possible from the lacrosse team. The last thing I needed was them smelling the remains of my day.

I sprinted down the steps and ditched the bag in the garbage room of the apartment building. Between the much-anticipated bowel evacuation and my own miraculous escape from having to explain myself to the lacrosse guys, I was walking on air. I felt great. Unfortunately, the feeling didn't last.

I figured the enema would have been the end of my journey through the world of shitlessness. It was merely the beginning. By that night I was once again stopped up, back to constantly feeling like I was about to shit only to find myself crying on the toilet because I couldn't.

To permanently correct my troubles, I was going to have to take things up to yet another level.

That's why I decided to get a colonic.

The next morning I went online and looked up different "colon hydrotherapy" clinics around New York City. Most cost about sixty bucks. The highest-end one I could find was $125. I immediately called that one. My thinking was that when it comes to having a high-powered suction machine connected to your asshole, you don't want to be a penny-pincher. The website for the place made it seem very new-agey, something I normally avoid like the plague, but I figured in this situation it might actually make sense for the whole place to be dedicated to soothing tones and colors, soft-spoken voices, and whatnot.

"Hello?" a man answered after just two rings of the phone.

"Hi," I said, feeling suddenly dirty. "I need a colonic as soon as possible, please."

"Okay," the man said. "Have you ever had one before?"

"I haven't," I answered. For some reason I felt like I was scheduling my first trip to see a call girl. And this man was a colonic pimp.

"It's going to feel so good," he assured me. "You will be completely aligned by the time it is over."

I didn't know what he meant by "aligned," but I was hoping it would correspond with my getting back to regular bm's.

I went to the clinic on a cold Saturday morning. I had to take off my shoes before entering. The lobby was filled with stones arranged in patterns on the floor, and there were three different fountains with small trees in them. Vaguely Asian music echoed throughout the building.

"We have a special today," the woman behind the counter told me. "Before your colonic, you'll be getting a free half-hour massage."

This worried me. *Had* I accidentally stumbled into a weird fetishistic prostitution ring? Was "$125 colonic" a code for entry into some sort of scatological sexual underground?

A frumpy woman wearing sweatpants and huge glasses emerged. She took me by the hand and led me into a massage room where candles glowed and soothing music played. She left so I could undress, then returned and gave me a deep massage.

I'd left my underwear on for safety's sake. Her massage was soothing. It was also very thorough. I couldn't tell if I was heading toward a hand job or if she was just a kindhearted hippie chick.

"We're done," she eventually whispered into my ear. "Take your time getting dressed."

She left. There was no happy ending, unless you consider a prolonged wait before someone eventually stuffs a tube up your ass happy.

After the massage, I was given a robe with no back and taken into a much more medical-looking room. There was a table set up next to a large, strange-looking machine. On the table was a coating of paper as well as an oddly thick cotton pad. A good-looking muscular black woman entered the room.

"If you need to use the bathroom," she said, "go now. Evacuate yourself completely." Her voice brimmed with confidence.

"I wish I could," I answered.

She stared me down. She was intimidating, but her eyes also burned with purpose. "Let's get you taken care of. Roll over onto your side."

"Hi, I'm Chris," I said as I followed her instruction.

"It's nice to meet you," she replied, all business. "You're going to feel some lubrication right now."

She lifted up my robe. I did indeed feel lubrication.

"Chris," she said, serious as a heart attack, "roll over onto your back. Be careful not to jostle loose the tube. Elevate your rear in the air."

I did as she commanded.

"Thank you for doing this," I said. "I've been having a bad week of indigestion."

"Chris, you don't need to thank me," she said. "This is my passion in life."

She pointed to the machine.

"I'm going to turn a light on over this tube," she said. "It will allow you to see all of the matter we remove from you today. Watching this debris exit your body will feel great."

This excited me greatly. The machine was turned on and all the air was sucked out of it so that when the water started traveling upward, it would not create any gas. My attendant turned, took my hand in hers, and spoke seriously, barely above a whisper.

"We're going to begin. I'm going to turn that switch. I will fill you with water," she told me. "The feeling will overwhelm you. When you feel like you are going to burst, say the word 'filled.'"

"I can do that," I assured her.

"After a few rounds with water," she said, "I'll fill you with chlorophyll. This will refresh your system while removing even more blockages. We'll repeat this process as many times as we must to clear you of blockages."

Her militaristic tone scared me and excited me at the same time. I was dealing with a true professional.

Now, I'm not going to compare a colonic with childbirth, or be presumptuous enough to say that having gotten one helps me to imagine what it must feel like to deliver a child. But what I will say is that I have no doubt it is as close as a man will ever come to knowing the sensations involved with that experience.

The machine was turned on, and within thirty seconds I was convinced that it was broken and that I was going to die. I felt so inflated with water that my assumption was the machine had locked in the "on" position, and that the woman in fact realized it was going to kill me. Rather than cause me panic, however, she was sparing me this information, likely so I might live my last moments on earth without being faced with the terrible knowledge of my own impending death.

"I'M FILLED UP!" I shouted. "PLEASE! PLEASE! I'M FILLED UP!"

"Chris, this will all be okay," the attendant shouted back over the rumble of the machine. Just when I thought I couldn't take another second, she reversed the flow and I got to see firsthand what had been blocking my insides for so long.

At first, only an extreme number of gas bubbles filled the tube. It disappointed me that I wasn't able to see any solid evidence of my near week of stomach pain. My attendant, who I believe was an angel sent from heaven to make people feel better in the tummy, began massaging my stomach from right side to left.

"I can feeeeel the blockage!" she shouted like a fiery Evangelical minister. "It's almost passing—I can feeeeel it!"

She pushed her fist hard into my stomach. That's when I saw it: dark, black, rock-hard chunks of shit shooting down a tube full of water. I reacted to this the same way women in movies do to their children being born—with utter joy and relief. I was physically spent, emotionally drained, and absolutely ready for the whole process to be over.

Unfortunately, it took over forty more minutes of being repeatedly filled with water and having my belly massaged to clear all the blockages. Over and over again the woman flipped the machine on. Over and over again I screamed in terror. Over and over she personally pushed lumps of poo out of me with her well-traveled fingers.

I'd just started getting accustomed to the sensation when the attendant mercifully informed me we were going to stop. The machine ground to a halt and I let out a sigh of relief. The odd thing is, once it was over I really felt like I'd accomplished something. The attendant's straight-laced demeanor broke and she smiled.

"I feel so good," I told her. "I feel so, so good."

"I know," she grinned at me. "Enjoy it."

Then she snapped back into military mode.

"Chris, let's focus up. Look, you've been apologizing a lot along the way," she told me. This was true. Every time I let out a chunk of shit or a big fart blast, I'd instantly apologized. This was because my mother raised me in such a way that if a grown woman is holding a tube firmly in your asshole and you let out a big fart in her face, you say you're sorry.

"And I have repeatedly told you it is my job, and I am very happy to help you," she continued. This was also true. She had been rooting for me the entire time.

"Now, what's going to happen next happens to *everyone*," she told me. "I do not want you to apologize for it. It is natural and therefore beautiful. Now do as I say. Roll back over onto your left side."

She placed the strange cotton pad I'd noticed before right under my butt. Shortly after, I felt her tugging on the tube and what happened next can only be described as a complete mess.

It was only in that moment that I truly realized how incredibly satisfying it can be, how absolutely free one can feel and completely in touch they can become—not just with themselves but with life itself—when they diarrhea onto the thinly latex-gloved hands of a stranger. In that moment I understood that the weird cotton pad had been there exactly for this purpose all along. This was all supposed to happen. As per my attendant's firm instructions, I wasn't embarrassed at all.

The attendant was all smiles. She breathed heavily, satisfied at a job well done.

"Now," she said, once again all business, "I want you to slip out of the robe you were wearing. You'll see that on the shelf above you is a fresh robe. Reach up and put that one on."

She paused, and took a deep breath.

"Whatever you do," she exhaled, "*under no circumstances do I want you to turn around and look at the condition of the robe you had on during the colonic.*"

I knew there must have been diarrhea everywhere—on the robe, on the table, who knew where else? I could not have been happier to follow her suggestion, and overall I couldn't have felt more grateful or better about the whole thing.

~~~

"I think the worst," my father said, "was the time you shit your pants at Six Flags Great Adventure."

"No," I said. "That wasn't the worst. That's not even in the top five."

My dad looked confused.

"Let me tell you what I did last month," I said. I sat down and told my parents all about my colonic.

"Well," my mother said when I finished speaking. "At least you apologized."

"Yeah," my father agreed. "At least we raised you right."

Jiu Jitsu

My breaths were coming fast and heavy. Maybe the panic was due to the fact that I was standing barefoot in an outfit resembling pajamas in public. Maybe it was the few hundred people shouting at me.

More likely it had something to do with the large bearded man standing eight feet away whose plan was to kick the living shit out of me. I glanced at the people all around me. I definitely didn't belong here. For a moment, I couldn't remember how this came to pass.

~~~

In 2004, I got a call from my old boss at *Weird NJ*. It'd been two years since I quit my job at the magazine to take a job in Los Angeles, and we'd spoken intermittently since then. It was good to hear from him. I'd feared that leaving on short notice had burned this bridge.

"We were wondering if you'd like to write a book for us," my boss said, much to my surprise. "It will be called *Weird NY*."

I was tasked with researching, writing about, and photographing any odd, haunted, or strange thing in the entire state of New York. I spent countless hours on the road, and experienced some very ill-advised situations. I almost peed my pants from fear in a cemetery in Frewsburg. I got lost looking for albinos in the woods outside of White Plains. In other words, it was the best job ever.

When the book was published in late 2005, I felt a great sense of accomplishment. But along with publication came a huge downside as I began to feel what I can only imagine empty-nest syndrome feels like. While the days immediately after the book came out were filled with excitement, after just a few weeks I found myself becoming restless and depressed. I had become used to having a huge project occupying all my time, and now without one I was bored and lonely.

I told myself I'd take a month before finding the next project to sink my teeth into. The plan was to use that month to get inspired again. So much for plans. One month off soon turned into six months of doing nothing but sitting around before I realized I was stuck in a major rut.

Then one day, as I was walking down Thirtieth Street in Manhattan in what had become my standard funk, I passed by a gym owned by legendary mixed martial artist Renzo Gracie. I'd once watched a fight of his on a Japanese DVD in which he refused to submit even after having his arm broken at the elbow. I recognized his name on the sign immediately and something told me I had to see a business run by a guy like that. I strolled into the building's lobby, and the doorman told me to head down a dimly lit set of stairs.

As I turned the corner at the bottom of the steps, I recoiled. The place reeked of man sweat. But even more overwhelming were the hordes of tattooed muscleheads wrestling on every inch of floor space. I felt as if I'd stumbled into a secret alternate reality I had absolutely no business being in.

I signed up for a year's worth of classes on the spot.

Jiu Jitsu is a martial art that revolves around joint locks; I was born with a joint disease. Jiu Jitsu relies on agility and maneuverability; I often trip for no reason besides the fact that walking eludes me. Jiu Jitsu is for the mentally and physically tough; I have the emotional stability of a pregnant woman, and physically, it would be kind to call me laughable.

But when it came down to it I was in a bad spot and needed to shake things up for myself. In that moment of what some would call clarity and others would call extreme foolishness, it seemed as though Brazilian Jiu Jitsu might just be the answer to all of my problems.

From day one, the training was far from easy. After my first class I sat in a corner dry-heaving. As the months wore on, I routinely limped through the other parts of my life due to the constant injuries I sustained. I received black eyes, horrific bruises, a popped bursar sac, and a rib that popped loose from its socket. All for a hobby I casually and voluntarily signed up for.

But I kept coming back. I'm sure some of it was rooted in my deep-seated sense of self-loathing, that I liked being beaten up. Most days, I'd show up, fumble my way through the lesson, then get severely thrashed during the sparring. Every once in a blue moon, though, I'd pull something off that would fuel the addiction. I'd sweep a guy off of me. I'd block him from doing a move he was going for. Every few weeks I'd even manage to get a guy to tap out to me. It was completely exhilarating.

Renzo himself once dropped by the gym and yelled some pearls of wisdom from the sidelines as we sparred.

"You spend most of your lives being the nail, my friends," he yelled one day as I was pinned underneath a very burly and very sweaty bearded guy. "But don't worry. One day, you'll be the hammer."

The few-and-far-between moments when I got to be the hammer validated all of the time I spent being the nail.

The mental trauma was actually worse than the physical. People at the gym found me funny, and this made things harder on me. It's rare for a Jiu Jitsu gym to take on a big-headed sad sack comedian as a student. Most of the dudes who do Jiu Jitsu are well built. Many have tattoos. I have one tattoo. It's Morrissey's signature. These guys had real tattoos, like the insignia of their former Marine battalion. There are some other nerdy guys, but the large majority of them are Asian, which gives them way more credibility as martial artists than I ever got. Every now and then you'd get some other weirdo like me, but they almost never stuck around.

The fact that some of the guys found my perseverance endearing was great, because they subsequently looked out for me. It was bad because the way they showed their affection was through tormenting me with no abandon.

The funniest guy at the gym was Black Rob. He was also the scariest. He's over six feet tall and around 250 pounds of pure muscle. When I met him he was a brown belt, right on the verge of getting a black belt (which, in the world of Brazilian Jiu Jitsu, usually takes well over ten years). Before Jiu Jitsu became his life, he'd served in the military and later as a cop. His entire adult life was based around violence. He looked like a badass on sight, and after talking to him for five minutes, I realized he was an even bigger badass than I could possibly imagine. Despite being incredibly intimidated by him, I'd spoken to him a few times in passing and cracked a few jokes that made him laugh. Still, I figured he had no idea who I was.

My first clue that this wasn't the case came while I was taking a class one afternoon. I was sparring another guy and we were really going at it. In our scuffle, my belt loosened and my gi jacket opened. My chest and stomach were exposed for the entire gym to see.

Black Rob had been eyeing my match from the side of the room. A lot of times the more experienced guys watched beginner classes to hand out advice to the novices. I made eye contact with Rob. He cleared his throat. I assumed he was going to drop a pearl of wisdom on me, something that would help me unlock the mysteries of Jiu Jitsu.

"What the fuck is wrong with your body?" he bellowed. "Are you a man or a boy?"

He was loud enough to make sure all of my classmates turned to see whom he was speaking about, and when they did, he cackled with glee. From that day forward, if I was training and Rob was around, I was heckled mercilessly for the amusement of others. The bright side was that other people were no longer allowed to fuck with me, but in exchange it meant that Rob could do whatever he wanted. I was, in effect, his prison bitch. Rob and I once sparred and it ended with him undoing my own belt and tying my hands together, laughing the whole time. I'd never felt more helpless in my life. And I was paying hundreds of dollars a month for this privilege.

Rob also wasn't the only person to develop a big brother/little brother system of teaching/torture with me. As I got more experienced, a black belt named Brian took me under his wing. He was a quiet, sort of nerdy guy who, despite being skinny and unassuming, was well known as one of the fiercest dudes in the school. If you were into mugging or murder or whatever and you passed this guy on the street, you wouldn't think twice about victimizing the shit out of him. But if you'd seen him fight even once for two minutes, you would sprint across the street in fear of his badassery.

Brian rooted for me as a fellow small guy and sparred with me to practice moves and let the rest of the gym know he was looking out for me.

Despite his mentorship, he didn't take it easy on me. One morning, he was working on judo throws and asked me to spar. I agreed. I'd sparred with him a handful of times before, and while it was tough and somewhat terrifying, I always walked away having learned something valuable.

We squared off and slapped hands as a sign of respect. I took a step forward and reached for his lapel.

Before my hand could get there, he grabbed my sleeve and twisted his body. I felt my own body leave the ground, and the next thing I knew, I was upside down and completely vertical. My head was even with Brian's head and my body extended straight out above me, my toes nearly brushing the ceiling. The sickening disorientation of this motion stopped only when I heard a loud thud. It took me a moment to realize that the thud was the sound of my own body slapping flat against the mat. I didn't reach this conclusion through analytical deduction, but instead via the feeling of sharp pain that washed over me due to the impact. I yelled. Yelling is frowned upon at the gym. It's a sign of weakness, and makes people skittish. I'd seen people dislocate their elbows and not yell. I promise you, though, this time I had no choice. I'd been thrown on many occasions before, but this happened so fast that I shouted out of instinct. It was the shout of a man who genuinely has no idea what the fuck just happened to him. The shock of hitting the ground was immense. I was still processing the fact that I had even left my feet.

Before I could fathom what happened, Brian twisted again. I didn't realize he was still holding his grips on me until I was again in the air, only now I was completely horizontal to the floor. He adjusted his foot positioning to send me downward and I hit the mat with an even more sickening thud. This time I didn't yell, but instinctively curled up into a tight ball. Brian stepped over me and executed a fierce arm lock that made me submit instantly.

In addition to the physical pain I was terribly confused. I rolled over and shook my head, clearing the cobwebs and wondering what the hell had just gone down.

Brian grinned at me. "You wanna talk about it?" he asked. The entire gym, all of whom had been watching his demonstration of skill, burst out laughing.

My least pleasant injury came when I was about a year into my training.

There was a tradition at the gym that took place whenever a new guy came to learn. If he was cool, humble, and wanted to jump into lessons, that was fine. No problems, and no questions asked. But not surprisingly, at a gym that teaches fighting you get a lot of testosterone-fueled lunatics who want to come in and kick everyone's ass right away. Those guys are usually thrown into the fire against someone with a little bit of experience. Guys like that need to be humbled. Once they are, they either turn into normal human beings and take classes, or they remain crazy and are sent on their way. Getting beaten is a litmus test to see just how agro these weirdo meatheads are.

Despite (and possibly because of) my size, some of the instructors really liked me and knew that I'd put in enough time at the gym to know—ever so slightly—what I was doing. So, on occasion, the teachers liked to use me as the experienced guy who faced off with the wild-eyed newcomers. After all, there is nothing better to prove the effectiveness of a martial art than losing to a dude who looks like me. On top of that, the teachers seemed to find it funny watching muscle-bound dudes with neck tattoos get worked up about not being able to beat me.

One afternoon, I was pitted against a very aggressive, brooding young man who weighed close to 300 pounds. Not 300 pounds of muscle, either—300 pounds of fat and bad attitude. I had immediate trepidations. Even with a year of experience, I still wasn't good at all. I was adequate at best. Usually in this situation, the teachers would face me off against some dude just a little bigger than me. I'd put him in some basic move he didn't know was coming, and he'd calm down. But this kid was different. Not only was he the biggest person I was ever asked to spar, something about his expression made him seem truly unhinged.

Our instructor matched us up and our grappling began. My opponent flailed all over the place, unable to control his movements. I remained calm, looked for an opening, and after a few minutes placed him in a triangle choke—a move that involved lying on my back and using my legs to cut off the supply of blood to the guy's brain. I had it locked in very tight.

Normally, the response to any locked-in submission move is to tap out and signal that you've given up. There's no shame in tapping out. I did it every day I walked into the gym. But this kid had a lot of ego and a lot of pride, and couldn't bring himself to admit defeat.

Before I knew it, the behemoth hoisted me into the air above his head. My instructor yelled, but the kid didn't pay any attention. He threw me down to the mat, putting his full 300 pounds behind him. I hit hard, and he came barreling down with me.

His head hit me in the front tooth and my entire top row of teeth went numb.

I stood, stared at him furiously, and walked off the mat. My instructor yelled at him some more.

Fuck, my teeth are gone, I thought. *There goes my acting career.* My mouth was so numb I couldn't feel how many teeth I'd actually lost.

A muscle-bound Brazilian came out of the other training room and looked at me.

"What happened, my friend?" he asked, gently.

"Y feeth," I said. "Got ocked in y feeth, on't know ow any gone." He placed his finger in my mouth.

"They're all there," he said. He yanked hard on my front tooth. "And they're still strong. That would have taken them out if they were coming out."

That man was Renato "Babalu" Sobral, the former light heavyweight champion of Strikeforce Fighting. Two nights later, he was knocked unconscious while fighting in the Ultimate Fighting Championships. I watched it on live TV and felt really bad about it. I also wondered exactly how my life had gotten to the point where I actually knew an Ultimate Fighter who had stuck his fingers in my mouth to make sure all my teeth were still there.

After about fourteen months at the gym, something I wasn't expecting happened: I got my blue belt. This is the second worst belt in Jiu Jitsu, but it was still more than I ever hoped to accomplish. There are few things I'm more proud of in life than that blue belt. The majority of guys who signed up for the gym quit before they got theirs, and every single one of them was more physically able to keep up than I was. The difference was I stubbornly and maybe even foolishly refused to quit, and I was rewarded for it.

Unfortunately, getting my blue belt also meant I was bumped up to the advanced classes. Now I was sparring the other blue belts, as well as the purples, browns, and blacks. I wasn't just in over my head. "In over my head" implies I still had a chance at coming up for air. This was more like a state of permanent drowning.

I once took a class where the other people *taking* the class included five UFC fighters, among them the legendary Georges St. Pierre. He was preparing to defend the UFC welterweight title later that week. I was preparing to audition for a role as a "guy who gets Cheerios thrown at his face" later that week. We very obviously represented the extreme opposite ends of the skill spectrum of the class.

Every day, I'd walk into the gym knowing I was going to get my ass beat. I'd get my ass beat. Then I'd leave, knowing that if I decided to come back the next day I would again get my ass beat. I'd come back the next day. And I'd get my ass beat. Repeat.

Somehow, though, I convinced myself I was getting better in spite of the beatings I took. After all, I was at one of the best gyms in the world, going up against some real monsters, and I kept coming back. While I was thrashed left and right, I rationalized that I had to be improving, and that in a less competitive environment I'd finally see my skills come to life.

So when I had the chance to sign up for a fight outside of the gym, I took it.

Once a year, my school holds a tournament. Students at all of the affiliate schools—those whose instructors studied under Renzo himself—are invited. Hundreds of people compete, and even more come to watch. I figured it was time to put my skills to the test.

Being smart was the only thing that ever helped me in Jiu Jitsu. Other guys could rely on strength and speed, but I had neither to fall back on. Any time I defeated a guy, it was because I was more focused than he was and made smarter choices than he did. So when the tournament was announced, my first attempt at outsmarting people was to cut weight.

At the time I was walking around at 155 pounds. I was in very good shape, but I knew that the other guys at my natural weight were all stronger than me, so I decided to cut down to the 135-pound weight class. I dieted for months leading up to the competition, eating only breakfast bars and cottage cheese. Within a few weeks, a physical transformation was visibly noticeable. At the same time I also decided to shave my head, telling myself I wanted to "look more like a fighter and less like a comedian." In reality, what I looked like was someone with a terminal illness.

Weigh-ins took place the morning before the tournament. The night before, I weighed myself at 147 pounds—still too heavy for my weight class. But this was intentional. The whole point of a weight cut is to drop all the water weight out of your body right before the weigh-ins. Water weight is very easy to put back on, so after the weigh-in you can actually regain a few quick pounds and fight at a weight much greater than the limitations of your weight class. I knew that if I could pull it off, I'd be fighting much smaller guys for once—an advantage I rarely ever held.

My friend Eugene is also into fighting, though he practices Muay Thai, the style of kickboxing founded in Thailand that involves kicking trees and shit. He offered to help me with the weight cut. The next morning, hours before the weigh-in, he and I went to the Russian baths in New York's East Village. As an extra measure, I rubbed a lotion called Albolene all over my body. The stuff is water based and opens up your pores, helping you sweat more. Wearing just shorts and covered in this goo, I stepped into one of the saunas.

The Albolene was a mistake. As soon as the heat hit my skin, my pores exploded and sweat covered me. I was soaking wet within minutes. The strain of the diet coupled with the water-weight expulsion had an immediate effect.

"You okay?" Eugene asked.

"Murrr," I replied.

"What?" He squinted at me with concern.

"Mmmmb," I grunted. I was too weak for words, too exhausted to explain. My eyes drooped, my head got heavy. After twenty minutes, Eugene dragged me back to the locker room.

I weighed myself. I was still a few pounds off, so we went back into the sauna. My lips were dry, my eyes hurt. I was soaking with sweat I could no longer spare. Mercifully, after just a few more minutes, he dragged me out of the sauna again. This time, my weight came in right at the limit.

We got dressed and I was too weak to even mumble. Every step I took required massive effort. Every movement of my head caused pain. We left the bathhouse and I recoiled at the sunlight. We walked to the corner so Eugene could get coffee.

"I'll be right back out," he said. "Then we'll get a cab."

I nodded. He stepped inside. I collapsed on the sidewalk. He came back out and hoisted me into a taxi. We headed to the gym.

At the weigh-in I stood in a long line of men far more physically impressive than I was. I made weight no problem. I'd lost twelve pounds in the twenty-four hours leading up to the fight, nine in the sauna that morning alone. I drank Gatorade, ate real food for the first time in weeks, and felt completely focused. Through my hard work and determination I'd given myself a leg up. That night I slept well, and when I woke up the next morning, my game face was on.

I showed up for the tournament at a high school gym in Bayonne, New Jersey, with ten of the pounds I'd lost back on my frame. The floor was covered in mats, upon which fights were set to take place all afternoon. It was ten in the morning, so most of the competitors weren't there yet, but the stands were already packed with spectators. Due to luck of the draw, my weight class and belt level was up first.

All of my possible opponents stretched in the warm-up area. I sized them up and felt great about it. They were tiny. My plan had worked. I was one of the bigger guys.

Or so I thought. As I finished stretching, a very confident-looking dude walked into the fenced-off area. He was significantly bigger than me and had a thick soul patch on his chin. I assumed he was there to help one of the competitors.

Trainers aren't supposed to come in here, I thought to myself. Then the dude sat down and stretched.

That motherfucker cut weight too! I thought. *And he did it way better than I did.*

One of the refs walked up to the entrance of the pen.

"Who's Chris?" he said. I stood and nodded. "And Tom." The big dude rose.

"You guys are up first." We looked at each other. I smiled. He did not. His eyes were completely devoid of emotion. I'd spent countless hours during the prior week mentally processing through moves and sequences, visualizing how this fight might go. I'd obsessively and nervously considered all my options. This guy's eyes demonstrated nothing but the cool confidence of a person who actually knows what he's doing. My stomach twisted. He walked past me onto the mat. I paused. I wasn't ready.

You're never going to be ready, I reminded myself. I took a breath and followed him.

Not only was I in the first weight class, I was in the first fight of the day. As I walked to the center mat, a roar broke out from the crowd. They'd been sitting and waiting in the uncomfortable bleachers for too long. Now the violence was finally about to begin and they were excited.

This monster whose name was apparently Tom stood across from me. His gi hung open and I could see he had a number of tattoos, as well as well-defined abs. I looked at his face and locked in on the most terrifying aspect of all. He. Had. A. Soul. Patch.

I'm fighting a guy who can grow facial hair, I thought. *I can't grow facial hair. Fuck, fuck, fuck.*

I was psyching myself out at a breakneck pace. The ref told us to walk to the center of the mat, where we shook hands. Then the match started.

He gripped my gi and I gripped his, and we battled for the takedown. The spectators cheered us on. No other matches had started yet, so their undivided attention was on us. This dude was strong. And confident. He had great posture. His grips were tighter than mine. Also, there was that motherfucking soul patch.

Still, he couldn't take me down.

I don't know if he was nervous too, or if his technique just wasn't there, but I realized he wasn't going to throw me. I calmed down and remembered one of my favorite moves: a sneaky judo throw where you use an unorthodox grip and trip your opponent.

I switched my grips and knew I had the move ready to go. He was a sitting duck.

But I hesitated.

I paused just long enough to second-guess myself and worry that the move wasn't going to work. Doubt, even if only briefly present, was death. I went for the throw and got into the correct position. I slid my foot around his in what would be the final step.

But then, halfway through the sequence, I bailed. My fear overtook me and I didn't commit fully to the move.

Tom picked up on the hesitation and acted fast. He grabbed my torso and threw me to the ground, hard. It wasn't pretty, but I can say firsthand it was really fucking effective.

From there I don't remember much, outside of being pinned down. My legs were positioned wrong. *Switch your legs!* I thought, but in my panic I didn't follow through on the impulse. At one point Tom went for an armbar, and I felt enough space to escape. But, again, I hesitated and allowed the moment to pass. Luckily, his technique was sloppy enough that he didn't finish me with it.

About a minute and a half into the match, he locked in another hold. When he fully committed to it, I tried in vain to escape. I rolled over my left shoulder and heard a sickening crack.

My own escape attempt popped my elbow out of its socket. From botching moves to overdoing escape attempts and injuring myself, I had defeated myself in every conceivable way. My arm went numb immediately. Unlike Renzo in the match I'd seen on DVD, I opted to stop fighting.

All my hard work in getting into the weight class was for nothing. All my illusions of having gotten better were proven false. I'd lost in less than two minutes.

But when I got off the mat, a wave of euphoria washed over me.

For me, as in all areas of life, Jiu Jitsu wasn't about winning or losing. It's about the fight itself. If it's about winning or losing, I'm fucked, because in all honesty, I tend to lose. I'm simply cut from that cloth. I've long accepted that having a name that spells "Get Hard" brings with it a certain loserish air.

But as long as I keep fighting, I'll be okay.

I thought about the book I'd published and how its completion had sent me into a tailspin. It didn't have anything to do with how the book turned out; it was that I no longer had deadlines I might miss. I no longer had to scramble to get photos taken. I no longer had the long arduous drives to find some remote haunted castle. For me, in the end it wasn't so much the outcome of the project as it was the fight to get it done.

With Jiu Jitsu, it was the same thing. But with a difference: it wasn't a onetime project. It was more like a continuous work in progress. Even if it was something I could never ultimately win, what's important is that it was a fight that I could keep going. No one likes losing. But as I've gotten older, I've figured out that winning brings with it its own baggage. Like a chicken sitting on a rock and hoping it will hatch, I think I'd rather fight forever.

Cross-Country

Driving, alone and unbothered, is the only way I can really slow down, stop, and think.

This was a realization burned into me during my days at *Weird NJ*. We had a big cargo van the company bought cheap that we used to deliver boxes of magazines all over the tri-state area. The air conditioning didn't work, it only had a radio, and it broke down often. I once single-handedly caused a traffic jam on Route 1 when the van broke down and I walked down the highway to get gas—and then back to the van—instead of calling a tow truck. The gas gauge was broken, so one never could tell. It turned out I wasn't out of gas, and while I sat in the driver's seat waiting for the tow truck I should have called in the first place, many drivers wished death upon me as they inched past my disabled vehicle.

But despite the headaches it caused me, during my most troubled days driving around in that van was my time to think, my time to process, my time to heal. Sitting in traffic on the Garden State Parkway, the hot summer sun beating down on the asphalt, the sweat from my back clinging to the dirty vinyl seat behind me—these were some of the best days of my life.

It sounds hellish, and it was, but there was something beautiful about it, too. Crisscrossing the highways of my home state gave me so much alone time. From mornings spent in the swamps of the Meadowlands, to afternoons spent driving through the farmlands off of Route 202, to late-day deliveries down the Jersey Shore followed by a scramble back north on the Turnpike to avoid getting stuck in traffic, being by myself, seeing things no one else was seeing, meeting people I might never meet again—something about this lifestyle helped me process my thoughts and get in touch with myself. While working at *Weird NJ* was often bizarre, the nonroutine of the place was the only thing that could make me feel normal.

Those were times of adventure that are pretty much long gone. I'm boring these days. Lately, a big accomplishment for me is getting my tax documents to my accountant. I can't think of the last time I missed an appointment, and I really haven't gotten into any trouble. I play basketball once a week with a bunch of professional tutors who vent about the kids they help. Worst of all, I find these stories about *tutoring* funny and exciting. When I recently discovered a restaurant in my neighborhood with six different soups on the menu I got real excited and texted my girlfriend. There's no question that the me from ten years ago would think of the me of today as a dreadfully boring dude. Soup would be the fifteenth most exciting thing on his agenda, at best.

I'm thirty years old and I'm starting to feel like it. Both physically, in that I can't play basketball without my knees hurting, and mentally, in that I'm starting to view the world through a less frantic, more sedate lens. I've come to accept that life is what it is. Anything I could have changed I changed long ago. The rest

of it I'm stuck with. Not that I've given up or become compla-
cent. I haven't and I'm not. It's just that I've begun to accept all
the things I don't have any control over and it's made life easier.

Another sign of getting old: whereas a few years ago I equated
the idea of getting married and having kids with a terrifying
death sentence that would kill all of my fun activities and dreams,
I'm now starting to see those things as *noble pursuits* that will kill
all of my fun activities and dreams. The fact that my friends are
all married doesn't bother me anymore. They're all popping kids
out and I've gone from being scared by that to being jealous of it.
It's all added up to the realization that while technically I'm still
not old yet, I'm actually looking forward to getting there.

Still, there are definitely times when I feel pent up, boxed in,
and worn out. The difference between now and my younger days
is that my reactions to those feelings are a lot less dangerous now.
My manic episodes are fewer and farther between, my anxiety
isn't triggered as easily anymore, and I can see my depression
coming a mile away and get prepared for it. As a result, I'm happy
a lot of the time now, and even when I'm not I tend to be content.

Even so, there are stretches when I just can't figure life out.
And when things get overwhelming, they hit hard and fast. More
often than not, I only have one solution. My therapist and I even
have a joke about it: shit is truly fucked up when I start threatening to take a road trip.

It must be something about all that soul-searching I did while
driving in my twenties, because now driving long distances always feels like the thing I need to do when I have to sort through
something. If I really can't figure out an issue in my life, my initial urge is to *drive cross-country by myself*. In fact, I have figured
out major life decisions this way. I am such a fucking weirdo that
the only way I can sort out the big problems in my life seems to

be by driving 3,000 miles, hoping I enter a Zenlike trance at some point along the way, and praying that the answers come to me if and when that happens. I'm sure there are cheaper ways to handle problems, ones that require less of a time commitment and allow you to stay in your home state; those methods just aren't for me.

Luckily, taking random road trips around the country has allowed me to see and experience the same sort of fucked-up shit I used to see and experience all the time when I was young. Maybe that's part of the catharsis. If anything, driving around America as much as I have has reassured me that I'm far from alone in my sad weirdness.

The first time I drove cross-country, my friend Nick and I wound up in Las Vegas. There, we met a man I know only as "Tumbleweed." He'd lived a few years in Queens as a kid, and had been friends with Nick during their middle school years. Now we were all adults, and even though Nick hadn't seen Tumbleweed in a long time, we decided to meet up with him. He showed us all over the non-Strip portions of town.

"Nicky, don't push your seat back," he said as soon as we got into his car. "There's a gun under there."

Things only got more intense from there. We saw all sorts of locals-only Vegas spots that night, but the real moments of beauty kept coming in the car. While driving us from one cocaine-addled off-Strip casino to another, Tumbleweed managed to say the worst thing I've ever heard another human being say. He was explaining to us that one of the perks of living in Vegas is that you get to date the strippers who pass through seasonally.

"I was fucking this one girl," he told me, barely keeping his eyes on the road. "She was like, 'Cum on my face, cum in my hair, cum on my tits.' I finally had to stop and be like, 'Bitch, I only got so much cum!'"

Tumbleweed was a sweaty, adrenaline-fueled madman. He said awful things about women, about life, about everything. Late that night, we headed to his car, which was on the top of a parking garage. Before we got out of the vehicle, Tumbleweed held his hand up to stop us. His voice dropped an octave. He stared wistfully through the windshield, where from the top of the garage we could see the desert unfold before us.

"What do you guys think would happen if I stepped on the gas right now?" Tumbleweed sadly said.

"We'd probably die, Tumbleweed," Nick answered.

"Yeah, Tumbleweed," I said. "Don't do that, Tumbleweed."

He didn't. Instead, we sat for ninety of the most uncomfortable seconds of my life staring out at the desert and the open sky. Tumbleweed threw the car into drive and took us back to our hotel. I've never spoken to him since, though we are Facebook friends. So far as I can tell via many pictures of him with overtanned ladies, things seem to be just about the same.

In 2009, I drove cross-country by myself, following the highways that replaced Route 66. Wherever remnants of the old road remained, I got off the interstate and followed those instead. There were pockets of dying roadside culture everywhere.

In the heart of Missouri, I passed what seemed to be an average house when I saw a sign posted out front reading "Live alligators, two dollars." I screeched to a halt and pulled into the gravel driveway.

Inside were endless jars of taxidermied creatures. Scorpions, lizards, spiders, and more floated in empty pickle jars, all up for sale. The place was dim and dusty. A heavyset woman leered at me from behind a counter as I perused the dead critters.

"Wanna see the alligators?" she smiled as I approached.

"I sure do," I said.

"JIM!" she shouted. "CUSTOMER!"

A rail-thin, strikingly tan man with a mullet unlike anything I'd ever seen in person emerged from the back room, wiping sleep from his eyes. He looked remarkably like a less tall and more meth-addled version of former major league pitcher Randy Johnson. Jim didn't say a word as I handed my two dollars over to the woman. He waved me toward him.

"Right this way," he said. I followed him.

"Wait," the woman said. "We got a few more."

A family entered the dead-animal shack. A short squat man with a shaved head and a goatee led the charge. His son sprinted off toward the dead-scorpion section despite the protests of his mother, an exhausted-looking woman who carried a screaming baby in her arms.

"Shiiiiit," the dad said as he handed over his money. "Two dollars? This shit better be good."

With that we were led to the backyard, where we passed a number of birds and a sleeping lynx in a tiny chicken-wire pen. *That doesn't seem like it should be legal,* I thought to myself, before looking back toward our mullet-headed guide and remembering that laws might not be so strict in this part of Missouri.

As soon as we were outdoors, the dad from the unruly clan who joined me took off his shirt, revealing both a beer belly and a number of tribal tattoos that wrapped around his sizable biceps. He walked straight toward me.

"What's your name?" he asked.

"Chris," I replied.

"I'm Mike," he spat out. "This is my wife Donna. That's my son Blue and my daughter Indigo."

"Hi, Donna," I smiled. "Hi, Blue."

Blue ignored me. I waved at baby Indigo. We turned a corner and there in front of us was an eight-foot-high chain-link fence. It was all that stood between us and four fully grown crocodiles.

They snorted and huffed, their eyes and snouts the only parts of them visible in the shallow muddy water they called home.

Mike grabbed the fence and shook it.

"Shit, this is a rip-off," he said. "For two dollars, I should be able to feed these motherfuckers."

The mullet head quietly nodded, then went back inside. Moments later, he emerged with a bag full of bloody meat. He unlocked the fence's gate and motioned toward all of us. Mike grabbed his preteen son's hand and dragged him away.

"Shit, you coming, Donna? What about you, Chris?" he bellowed as he ducked into the crocodile pen.

"I'm good," Donna said. "You go ahead, baby."

"I'm good too, Mike," I said. "You guys have fun."

"Huh," Mike snorted, looking me up and down condescendingly. "Okay." He rolled his eyes at my lack of bravery.

For the next three minutes, I assumed I was going to witness the death of Blue. His dad taunted the crocodiles, yelling at them, throwing meat at their heads. Blue sprinted around with all the fervor and enthusiasm of an ADD-stricken child who has never been disciplined while his dad did everything he could to enrage crocodiles purely for the fun of it.

Somehow, the animals restrained themselves and chose not to eat this antagonistic man or his troubled son. Mike and Blue emerged from the cage.

"Shit," Mike said. "I feel like a fucking man right now, dog."

We continued through the backyard, where we next came upon two full-grown tigers standing on a hill enclosed by more chain-link fencing. Mike sprinted ahead, screaming, then grabbed the fence and shook it.

"What the fuck?" he screamed a few feet away from a bored-looking tiger. "Try something, bitch! Come and get me!"

The mullet head grabbed his shoulder and pulled him away.

"Bullshit," Mike mumbled before spitting on the ground.

Last but not least was a full-grown male lion, tucked away in a corner of the yard. He sat lazily in a corner of the too-small concrete pen he lived in.

"You gotta let me play with it, bro," Mike begged the mullet head. "You gotta."

"Can't do it," the mullet head drawled. "We used to play with him when he was a kid. He thinks he can still do it. Fucker doesn't know his own strength. Now he plays with people, he just fucking kills them. It sucks."

Mike was disappointed. I, on the other hand, was fine with the decision.

On another trip, I found myself deep in Texas when I got trapped in a lightning storm due to my own stupidity. It never occurred to me that driving through a storm in Texas might be a little different from driving through one in my home state of New Jersey. In Jersey, people slow down for the first ten minutes of a storm, then proceed as per usual. But Texas storms don't fuck around. When lightning bolts started hitting the actual highway I was driving on, I figured it was time to pull off and find a place to spend the night. Unfortunately, every hotel I stopped at was all booked up, presumably by the rational people who had pulled off the highway when they saw the deadly electrical storm looming in the distance.

I wound up sitting in a dusty truck stop diner all night, eating a not-great grilled cheese sandwich. My waitress was a teenaged Mexican American girl. The hostess was her younger sister. They'd seated and served me in silence, but after I'd waited about an hour for the storm to pass, my waitress meekly approached me.

"Your accent ain't from around here," she said, her own accent more Valley Girl than either Texan or Mexican.

"I grew up in New Jersey," I said. "I live in New York now."

"Oh my God," she said, her eyes growing wide. "Are you SERIOUS?"

"I am," I smiled. For the next fifteen minutes, no matter what I said, she shouted the words "Are you SERIOUS?" in response.

She asked me every question she could about New York. It all culminated in something I didn't see coming. After her first dozen questions, she got nervous and shifted back and forth on her feet. She looked back at her sister, who nodded, egging her on.

"I gotta ask," she said. "Have you ever seen Ground Zero?"

"I have," I said, suddenly serious. Having been in the tri-state area on 9/11, I felt a strange responsibility to convey the experience to this young girl in an appropriate way. My mind scrambled as I tried to figure out what to say about that day, but before I could think of anything, she interjected.

"Oh my God, are you SERIOUS?" she said. "You are so *lucky.*"

I was shocked.

"Not really," I said.

"Why not?" she asked.

"Well, it's kind of the worst thing ever," I said. Then I smiled. She smiled back, not understanding at all what I meant. Satisfied, she went back to whispering with her sister and ignored me for the rest of the night.

On another trip across Texas, in early 2011, I had a short but sweet encounter that summed up everything I love about the great Lone Star state. I'd stopped for gas in a dusty little town off of a two-lane highway, and when I stepped inside the station to pay I saw that they had a whole bunch of kitschy items for sale. Among them was a red baseball hat with a picture of a deer on it.

That's the coolest hat in the fucking world, I thought to myself, clearly affected by road delirium. It had been a few days since I'd been able to shower, and so in addition to appreciating

the awesomeness of the hat I was feeling pretty grungy and figured that using it to cover up my unwashed hair wasn't a bad
idea. I paid for it and put it on. As I left the store, a wiry, grizzled
old local entered.

"Damn, boy," he said. He grinned a toothless grin at me and
pointed at the hat. "You about to go get your redneck on?"

"I'm gonna do my best," I said, before strolling out. I've never
felt more American, more like a man, in my entire life.

During another trip driving from California to New York in
2009, I made a foolish mistake in my trip planning. I forgot that
Indiana occupies a strange place in space-time. It is a state pop-
ulated by insular farmers who play by their own rules, and those
rules don't involve recognizing daylight saving time.

I'd pushed hard that night, intent on driving until 4 A.M. before stopping, in an effort to get home fast. Due to my mistake
with the time zones, I drove until 5 A.M., costing myself an hour
of sleep. Worst of all, by the time I went to pull over I couldn't
find an open hotel room for miles. The first five places I stopped
at were sold out. I was on the verge of sleeping on the side of the
highway in my car when in a last-ditch effort I rolled into the
parking lot of a crappy roadside motel.

The guy behind the counter was a smooth-looking black guy
with a pony tail.

"How can I help you?" he asked, a broad knowing grin on his
face. He tapped the counter in front of him excitedly, displaying
a large number of rings adorning his well-manicured fingers.

"I need a room," I said. "Haven't been able to find one tonight. I'm pretty exhausted."

"I got one room open," he said, looking slightly confused.
"It's a suite though. Ninety bucks."

"That's fine," I said. "As long as I can crash for a few hours,
I'll pay anything."

I filled out the paperwork and he handed me my key. I went to my car to get my bag. I headed back inside, wanting nothing more than to sleep.

When I got to my room, the guy who had checked me in was inside.

"Sorry, sorry!" he yelled when I yelped in fear. "I just wanted to make sure no one was in here." He scurried away.

I was confused, and couldn't quite piece things together in my exhausted state. I entered the room and saw that a gigantic red heart-shaped hot tub took up most of the space. A king-sized bed with an attached coin-operated vibrating machine stood next to it.

I sat on the bed and ruffled my brow. It took me only a few minutes of shaking off my exhaustion to realize I was sleeping in a hooker hotel. In the last open room. Which had probably been rented hourly up until that point in the night. The man was probably making sure no hookers were practicing their wares on the bed I was about to sleep in.

I took a nice hot bath in the heart-shaped tub and slept for three uncomfortable hours.

Through all my soul-searching travels across the country, I've met a lot of strange people. I've been lost in a lot of interesting places. I've seen things I never thought I'd see, done things I never thought I'd do.

These trips have always made me feel better, but usually I don't even realize it until the very end. It's when I'm back in New Jersey, exhausted and making my way past the flame-dotted refineries along the Turnpike, with planes flying too low over my head on their way into Newark Airport, that it happens. It's then that I know that I'm home.

The trips I take may make me feel better, but they still don't make me feel like I'm "okay." One of the things I've finally accepted is that I'm not sure I ever will. I don't know if Tumble-weed, Mike, Blue, Indigo, Donna, the girl from Texas, or that hotel clerk in Indiana are okay, either. From my earliest days in West Orange to my travels in California, I don't know if I've ever met anyone who is.

But I do know I feel better when I'm home. Where my memories of Pa and Koozo collide, where I became a young man and where I lost my mind in the process, where I grew up and got better, I'm home. Maybe not okay, but home.

Acknowledgments

The author would like to thank the following for their support, guidance, and inspiration: Ken and Sally Gethard, Gregg and Ilana Gethard, Fran Gillespie, Ethan Bassoff, Jonathan Crowe, Brian Stern, Dianne McGunigle, Joe Mande, Anthony King, Will Hines, Shannon O'Neill, everyone at the UCB Theater, *Nights of Our Lives*, *Asssscat*, the cast and crew of *The Chris Gethard Show*, and the entire down-the-hill section of West Orange, New Jersey.